AT THE SOUND OF HIS VOICE

Pamela A. Jones

At the Sound of His Voice
Copyright© 2019 by Pamela Jones
Thousand Oaks, CA 91360
pjgraceandglory@gmail.com

PRAISES FOR *AT THE SOUND OF HIS VOICE*

Recognizing the myriad of ways God impresses his wisdom and purpose into our hearts makes our faith come alive. Pamela A. Jones in *At The Sound of His Voice*, shares from her experiences and her journals how God makes himself known to her. The simplicity and authenticity of her life will inspire you to do the same.

Wayne Jacobsen
Author, Speaker
Author of *HE LOVES ME* and co-author of *THE SHACK*

If hearing from God has always baffled you, this book is a key to unlock the mysteries. In *At The Sound of His Voice,* Pamela A. Jones brings us along on her own wonderful journey of getting to know God and hearing His voice clearly. In my 40 years as an author and Bible teacher, I can truly say this is one of the most honest, refreshing, hopeful books I've seen. Once you start reading, you won't be able to stop!

Karen Jensen Salisbury
Author, Speaker
www.karensalisbury.org

Jesus said, "The words that I have spoken to you are spirit and are life" (John 6:63 NASB). What I love most about *At the Sound of His Voice* is that Pamela Jones has included prophetic revelation she received from Jesus Himself. In each and every chapter, we are blessed with Heaven's perspective on the topic discussed providing an eternal, transcendent point of view. What a gift! I recommend this devotional book, as I know it will be an encouragement in your walk with the Lord. Best of all, I hope it inspires you to begin having two-way conversations with Jesus because *His* words are life!

Dr. Charity Kayembe
Founder of GloryWaves.org
Co-author of *Everyday Angels* and *Hearing God Through Your Dreams*

If you passionately pursue living from the sound of His voice, this book is a must read and a powerful addition to your library. I know the power of His voice and I know Pamela A. Jones. The two have come together to provide a life changing manuscript for those hungry for more.

Reggie Mercado
Sr. Leader
The Fountain, Moorpark, CA.

This book is an excellent example of *logos* and *rhema* flowing together. You get a Scripture verse and then God speaks about the application of that verse to one's life. Jesus said, It is the Spirit who gives life; the flesh profits nothing. "The words (*rhema*) that I speak to you are spirit, and they are life" (John 6:63).

Dr. Mark Virkler
President
Communion With God Ministries

Pamela A. Jones is one of the most gifted, creative, godly women I know. Her reflections and revelatory dialogues with the Lord shared in this book are amazing, and reveal His perspective on so many key topics that concern every believer. I encourage you to read slowly and meditatively, as you take in the depths of His wisdom and love as revealed to His daughter, Pamela.

Norma Letinsky
Professor Emeritus and
Kingdom Partners ministry

Pamela beautifully reveals a pearl in this book — something of value. It allows the reader to hear the sound of His voice.

Barbara Peters
Chairman, International Children's Aid Network (ICAN)
President/Founder of Special Ops Woman Ministries

DEDICATION

To my family, who are my heart and home on earth.

To my Dad and Mom, who now abide in their heavenly home. They instilled in me the values that made me the person I am today.

To my children, Jessica and Paul, who have given me the opportunity to grow a mother's heart, without which I would not have experienced such depths of joy and fulfillment in life.

To my siblings, Claudia, Teri, Milt, and Steve, who make me laugh and cry, and make me proud to be their big sister.

I love you all!

ACKNOWLEDGEMENTS

I acknowledge my Heavenly Father and the gifts He has given me. I bow to my Lord and Savior Jesus Christ. I daily appreciate the Presence of the Holy Spirit leading and guiding me into all life and godliness.

My sincere appreciation goes to Dr. Mark Virkler and his tireless dedication to teaching how to hear the voice of God. Without his instruction and resources, this book would never have been written.

I am truly grateful to my friends Catherine Alvarez, Norma Letinsky and Mary Weyand, whose editing skills and suggestions for content greatly enhanced this work.

Finally, to all my prayer partners (too numerous to mention) who lifted up this project — a heartfelt thank you!

CONTENTS

FOREWORD
By Dr. Jeannette Storms

The voice of God whispers, and sometimes, even shouts, in the realness of everyday life. It is not reserved only for the super-spiritual or for monks, nuns and otherworldly people. It can come unexpectedly or as a result of desperately seeking God. It often comes during the depths of pain or in the midst of solving a massive problem. God speaks not only in crisis, but also in our quiet times with Him. Perhaps these whisperings of the Divine are more poignant and affirming than the times when He speaks during times of stress, disappointment and dislocation. This book invites you to journey with a woman who has lived these moments and wants to share them with you.

Please, know that the Creator God who took time again and again to speak in the stillness or the storm to her is close to you as well, and desires a friendship with you. If you are already his friend, then her journey will challenge you to listen more intently and to believe that he can and will speak. The Creator who spoke the worlds into existence still speaks. His voice is one of authority, gentleness, wisdom and kindness. Stop and listen! Look up and see what He is communicating, whether through the clouds or in a vision.

Written by a dear friend who has lived in close and intimate relationship across time, this book will open new avenues for you to hear from God. Based on her real life experiences, it will help you discover new ways of hearing from God whether through the Word, the inner whisper of His voice or visions. However God chooses to speak, it is always special. The unique organization of the book makes it a handbook that you can access again and again. When you find yourself wanting to be in control, or discover you have a hard heart, or are in need of healing, you will find words the Lord spoke to Pamela that you can apply to your own situation.

Above all, please know that the same Lord Jesus Christ who spoke to her still speaks and wants to say something to you, just as he did to her.

Dr. Jeannette Storms
Founder and President of Kingdom Connexion
and Professor Emeritus

INTRODUCTION

Have you ever contemplated the majesty of creation and wondered if the Creator is still involved in the universe He created, or is He just sitting unengaged on a throne far, far away? Can He see us? Does He hear us? Would He actually speak to us? In reality, God is a Speaking Spirit. In Genesis, the Book of Beginnings, we are introduced to His Voice as He calls all things into existence. Every word that He spoke created the endless heights and depths of the heavens and the earth. We are told in the Gospel of John that the full expression and the personal manifestation of God's voice is the *logos,* the Living Word. According to the book of Hebrews, all things continue to be upheld, propelled and maintained by His word of power:

> The Son is the radiance and only expression of
> the glory of [our awesome] God [reflecting God's
> Shekinah glory, the Light-being, the brilliant
> light of the divine], and the exact representation
> and perfect imprint of His [Father's] essence,
> and upholding and maintaining and propelling
> all things [the entire physical and spiritual
> universe] by His powerful word [carrying the
> universe along to its predetermined goal].
> Hebrews 1:3 (AMP)

Psalm 29 decrees that the voice of the Lord is so full of majesty that it thunders through the skies. His powerful voice breaks the cedars of Lebanon and causes the deer to give birth. According to Psalm 103, His angels (who excel in strength) heed and do the voice of His word. So imposing is His voice that it causes the earth to melt like wax. From beginning to end, the Bible is replete with examples of God speaking to priests, prophets, kings, and all manner of creatures great and small. For He alone knows the frequency and resonance of all creation.

Then should we, God's children, expect to hear His voice? When God created man in His image and likeness, and then, Face to face, breathed the Spirit of Life into his nostrils, some translations say that man became a speaking spirit. Our Creator communicates with us Heart to heart, Spirit to spirit, deep within the recesses of our being. We His children should indeed be able to hear His voice. In fact, when the Living Word walked the earth, He said that He was the Good Shepherd Whose voice the sheep would know and follow.

This book is a glimpse into my journey following the voice of God in my own heart. It is a humble attempt to share the insights, wisdom and counsel that I have received and recorded as I listen to the sound of His voice within. It is my sincere desire that these excerpts will inspire you to find your own journey, and the thrill of the sound of His voice for you.

PROLOGUE

I have long been fascinated with the sound of God's voice. What could a sound that has enough pervasive power to produce something out of a vast nothingness be like? The diversity of His audible expression that captivated me came from a variety of scriptures. The beginning of the book of Genesis, which tells the story of the creation, is one. Also, the Gospel of John, in the first chapter, talks about how the incarnate Christ is the personal expression of God as the Living Word. However, the selection of scripture that inspired me to choose the title of this book comes from Psalm 29. This selection is from the Good News Translation:

The Voice of the Lord in the Storm
[1]Praise the Lord, you heavenly beings;
  praise his glory and power.
[2] Praise the Lord's glorious name;
  bow down before the Holy One when he appears.
[3] The voice of the Lord is heard on the seas;
  the glorious God thunders,
  and his voice echoes over the ocean.
[4] The voice of the Lord is heard
  in all its might and majesty.
[5] The voice of the Lord breaks the cedars,
  even the cedars of Lebanon.
[6] He makes the mountains of Lebanon jump like calves
  and makes Mount Hermon leap like a young bull.
[7] The voice of the Lord makes the lightning flash.
[8] His voice makes the desert shake;
  he shakes the desert of Kadesh.
[9] The Lord's voice shakes the oaks
  and strips the leaves from the trees
  while everyone in his Temple shouts, Glory to God!

¹⁰ The Lord rules over the deep waters;
  he rules as king forever.
¹¹ The Lord gives strength to his people
  and blesses them with peace.

It is magnificent to me that the same voice that thunders without to maintain the pulsating universe in order, is at the same time the tender voice that whispers within to bless and bring His people peace.

There are many ways to hear the sound of His voice. The most dependable and the primary vehicle is the Bible itself. When we read, study, or listen to an audio version of the Bible, it is God speaking to us. He and His Word are the same — inseparable. The same Holy Spirit Who inspired the many writers to pen those sixty-six books of the Bible is the same Holy Spirit Who will illuminate and interpret its truths to our hearts and minds.

God can and will speak to us through pastors, teachers, counselors, and others who have studied to minister the wisdom of God as their profession. He is a Speaking Spirit who created us in His image and therefore is always in pursuit of intimate conversation with us. I have learned to never limit His voice to just the professional grown-ups, however. God has spoken to me through family, friends, coworkers, and even small children in a most profound way.

I have heard God speak to me through movies, TV commercials, billboards, car license plates, and the great outdoors — wind, sea, clouds, trees, mountains. When I contemplate the macrocosm and microcosm of nature, from the gargantuan galaxies to the subatomic particles of power, I can scarcely grasp the grandeur of His wisdom in speaking all of creation into existence. Even the stars sing in the heavens to Him.

We read in the Bible that God spoke through a donkey, and through angels. I do not believe there is a limit to His avenues of conversation with us. For the purposes of this book, however, I have chosen to only highlight the still, small voice within our spirits. It is so gentle, spontaneously bubbling up from within, that it is easily missed in our culture of the loudness without.

God can also speak to us through dreams and visions. When you consider that we sleep approximately one third of our lives and have our defenses down during that time, it is probably the perfect moment for the Almighty to get a word in edgewise! Visions can be on several levels, but suffice it to say that they are a function of our imagination directed by the Holy Spirit. Both of these avenues are usually symbolic and very personal to the individual.

In this writing, I will share some of the visions that I have had. I just want to clarify that when I use the term *vision*, it simply means that I see something like a mini-movie playing across my mind as I yield my imagination to the Holy Spirit. It is much like having a daydream when the mind wanders off into a scenario, and plays something out in our imaginations.

The reason that I have chosen to share a few of my visions is because these pictures that have played across my mind during my devotional time with the Lord are the language of the heart. The language of the mind is ideas, but the language of our hearts - or spirits, is pictures. When we become children of God by being born of God in the spirit, the Holy Spirit takes up residence in our hearts. When Jesus walked on the earth, He used parables or picture stories to make truth relevant in people's hearts. The Holy Spirit does the same thing today for us. He reveals truth in our hearts through pictures so that truth may become reality in our lives as we see it, ponder it, understand it, and embrace it.

As you begin reading, take your time. This book is not necessarily designed to be read from front cover to back cover. It is simply arranged in alphabetical order by topic. Rather, it is like a menu from which you select a meal that you would enjoy. Some topics may be like an appetizer, while other topics may be more like the main course. It is my sincere desire that whatever you select, you would be fed in spirit and soul. Choose a topic that draws you in, take a seat, relax, and savor every morsel. Allow the One Who loves you to nourish you with His voice.

The following portions of the book in *italics* are excerpts from the journals that I have been writing since 1980, so are not necessarily current. Rather, they are what I perceived to be the voice of God speaking to my heart over the past 40 years. All references to Almighty God are capitalized.

Whispers of the Divine

Truly you have heard My voice speaking to you — more than you know. Because of the discipline in your life at this time, you are able to integrate My voice into the flow of your days. This is and has been My desire for all of My people, and I long for the day when My voice will be an uninterrupted flow in the hearts of My people. Those who are still enough to listen can hear Me now. There are many distractions, and it takes discipline to quiet oneself enough to hear me. I AM the still, small voice. Not small in power, but small because it is so deep within and compared to the noise without it seems very distant and small. However, to those who are willing to pay the price, it is a power to be reckoned with as you have learned this day. And your voice, too, when directed by My Spirit is a power to be reckoned with. So, I encourage you today to obey what you have learned and choose wisely how to use your voice. It is a creative or destructive force.

VISION: I imagine the throne of God and see the energy of His being above the throne almost like pulsating Northern lights. Every time He speaks, the waves of the energy of His voice go all the way out to the edge of the expanse of the universe, and into the depths of the tiniest particle of the microcosm of atomic power. The power of His voice reaches to highest heaven and lowest hell. There is no place that His voice doesn't go when He speaks. There is enormous radiating power in His voice — power in the voice of the Almighty. It makes me want to say only what He says so that His power will be released when I speak.

Chapter One

COMPARISON

Comparison is the thief of joy.
—Theodore Roosevelt

Trouble in Paradise

When Jesus walked the earth, He frequently taught life lessons through parables; instructing principles in the truth through relatable pictures found in everyday experiences. By the conclusion of each story, there was always a challenge to assess one's own response to the situation being illustrated. Sometimes, life itself brings us vivid parables to highlight a crack in our armor pointing out a lesson that we need to learn. Allow me to recount one such modern day parable.

Marty and Maureen had been married for thirteen years, and their relationship was growing increasingly tense. They decided to go to Hawaii on a second honeymoon to try to rekindle their affection for each other. They needed to reconnect and take a break from the demands of work, raising children, ministry, household duties, and financial concerns. What better place to rest and hit the reset button than paradise itself on the islands of Hawaii? However, by the third day, it had become evident that even paradise could not dissolve the mounting tension that had accumulated in the marital relationship.

One particular day was spent on the big island of Hawaii hiking around the volcano craters, lava tubes and steam vents. By evening, the weary pair was erupting at each other in anger and hostility, spewing out so many hot and searing words. Steaming like the open shafts of the earth, they were emitting sulfurous, stinking odors of bitterness, hatred, and other vile emotions. And like the burning lava, they retired to separate beds, becoming dark, hard, and crusty like volcanic formations in the night.

Do you ever feel like you're comparing yourself to or competing with your spouse? Perhaps you feel that you are putting more effort into the relationship than your partner. Over the course of a marriage, anyone may sometimes feel overlooked and underappreciated. Some may view their marital division of responsibilities as inequitable. Such comparison leads to a fracturing of the union. The partners in a healthy marriage (or any relationship) should complement each other rather than compete with one another.

There is truly only one power with enough erupting goodness to heal and resurrect a marriage in trouble, or any other relationship, and it cannot come from human energy or effort. It can only come from the power of God's love.

Whispers of the Divine

Each time you have compared your life to the lives of My other children, and have examined their blessings in the light of your wants or needs, you have lived less loved. Comparison to others always leads to feeling less loved because it is not an accurate measurement of My love for each unique individual. Only I know the hearts of men, and what they receive or do not receive in the context of My blessings. It is more a factor of their receptivity and faith than My ability and love. In actuality, there are many factors that go into receiving blessings — it is as complex as it is simple, but it is never to be a measurement of My love. All of My blessings are available to all of My children.

Sometimes you are jealous when you think that I am treating others with more honor than I treat you, and you become angry. Remember Cain's response to my acceptance of Abel's sacrifice? And remember Esau's response to Jacob when he found that his father had blessed him with his own birthright? Do you remember the jealousy the older brother had for the younger brother in the story of the prodigal? Remember how Joseph's brothers sold him into slavery because they hated that their father favored him? All of these are examples of jealousy when one feels undeserving of love by the Father. I have made it abundantly clear that I don't prefer any one of My children more than the others, but sometimes one can accept My love more readily, and there seems to be more of a blessing. The truth is that I have given to all of My children the same blessings in My Son Jesus. Some more readily receive.

Comparison is a ploy of Satan that he has been using since the Garden of Eden. Satan's iniquity was first conceived when he, as Lucifer, fell into comparison, because he wanted to be like Me — only greater, which is also pride. This is a deadly sin because it disables you from being thankful, grateful and able to receive from Me. It also can lead you to obtain what you want apart from Me. The world operates on the basis of this, but you must not. First of all, you must be thankful for who you are individually as I have created you, and most definitely do not compare yourself to others. I am a Creator of unique design. Just look around you in nature — the birds, the flowers, the trees, the creatures big and small are all unique. You wouldn't think of comparing an elephant to a dog, or a rose to an iris, or a pine to an oak tree — how much more unique are those who I have made in My own image and likeness! Be grateful for who you are, because My design of you has been deliberately planned for your best self. Yield to all of who you are as I have created you in your spirit, and soul and body, and do not disparage any part of yourself. Only then can you be free to be yourself. Allow others the freedom to be who I have created them to be and celebrate your differences. Encourage others in their unique design. This is true freedom.

Chapter Two

COMPASSION

There never was any heart truly great and generous, that was not also tender and compassionate.
— Robert Frost

Finding a Treasure in the City Dump

Have you ever gone treasure hunting? I never have, but I have watched programs where people sail the seas searching for sunken ships with all kinds of treasure. During the Gold Rush days, many folks were lured out West by the possibility of finding golden nuggets that would make them rich. Maybe when you were a child like me, you played pirates and pretended to have a map with an X that marked the spot of buried treasure.

The Bible is full of stories about all sorts of treasures, but did you know that God talks about treasures of darkness[1] in His Word? The treasures He is talking about are not gold, silver, gems, or other such items. I found out what He considers treasures one day at the Mexico City dump when He allowed me to go with Him on His treasure hunt.

Several times in my life I have had the great honor and privilege of going on mission trips. One of the most memorable was a mission trip to Mexico City. I was invited to work with a team of missionaries who had started a church and Bible training center. A sequence of miracles of divine connections and intervention occurred before and during that trip.

Prior to leaving, I had saved up several thousand dollars to go on the trip. Then, just two days before I was due to fly down to Mexico City, I found out that I owed a significant amount in taxes. The tax debt was exactly the same amount that I had saved up for my trip.

My heart sank when I realized that if I paid the taxes, I would then not be able to go on the mission trip. I went to the Lord in prayer about this situation, and I felt that He spoke to me two words of instruction from the Scriptures. The first was from John 17:23, and the second was from Matthew 17:24-27. In essence the message God was giving me was that He loves me as much as He loves Jesus, and since He paid Jesus' taxes supernaturally, He would also pay my taxes supernaturally.

On the basis of my faith in His Word, I paid my taxes with the money I had saved for my trip, and then subsequently money miraculously began to come in for my trip just one day before I was supposed to leave. When I arrived in Mexico, I expected to have to pay for room and board, but instead God provided a gracious and wealthy family who put me up for five months without asking for anything in return. They considered it a blessing to have a missionary in their home.

I probably could write a whole book just on my experiences during those five months in Mexico City, but what I want to tell here is one story in particular that profoundly moved my heart.

Our team planned one outreach to the city dumps in Mexico City. The city dumps, or *basureros* as they are called, are miles wide and acres deep with all kinds of trash and garbage. There are very poor people who work and live in the city dump in homes that they construct of the debris found at the dump. They, of course, have no electricity or running water or any amenities at all.

On our visit there to share the love of God, I noticed a gentleman standing off by himself to one side. I went over to him and began to speak to him about the hopes and dreams and plan that God had for his life. He shared with me that he wanted to be a worship leader. I prayed with him before we left.

Here is the miraculous part. I had been so touched by this gentleman's dream of becoming a worship leader, that several weeks later I was persuaded that we should go back to the dump and invite him to accept a scholarship to attend the Bible training center. Please understand that the *basureros* were a couple of hours away by taxi or bus, and the dump itself was so vast that it would be virtually impossible to find anyone in the miles and mountains of trash. However, when God is in pursuit of a soul, his love is relentless and never fails!

When we arrived at the dump, we asked someone if they knew this gentleman, and they did in fact know him. They went out to look for him while we waited for quite a while. Eventually he found us, and we had a chat inviting him to become a part of the school where he could be trained to be a worship leader. He was thrilled, and was able to begin his journey in fulfilling his dream. We were moved by the amazing love and compassion of God for every human being on the planet. He knows you. He knows where you live, and He knows your heart and your hopes and dreams! He has a plan and purpose for every person's life! You are His treasure!

> I will give you the treasures of darkness And hidden riches of secret places, That you may know that I, the Lord, Who call you by your name, Am the God of Israel.
>
> Isaiah 45:3

Even though this verse is addressed to Persian King Cyrus and does refer to a hidden physical treasure, it can also refer to those in spiritual darkness.

Whispers of the Divine

When you have the compassion that I have for people then you will see the miracles I saw. You will do the miracles I did because the compassion of God releases the power of God to action.

Chapter Three

CONTROL

Today I know that I cannot control the ocean tides. I can only go with the flow.
— Marie Stilkind

Who's in the Driver's Seat?

Have you ever known someone who didn't know how to stay in his or her lane? Living in the greater Los Angeles area gives me the opportunity to drive some of the busiest freeways in the entire world. There are people driving on these eight to ten lane mega freeways who choose to weave in and out of lanes, sometimes crossing over several lanes at a time. They act like they own the road. This makes for hazardous conditions for the rest of us who stay in our chosen lane most of the time, until we politely signal to change lanes.

I enjoy doing water aerobics in the community pool at our condominium complex. We have a nice, L-shaped pool that is equidistant on both the vertical and horizontal sides of the "L." I like to take the bottom end of one side and do my laps back and forth in that one lane. Protocol for doing laps in a pool is to pick a lane and then stay in that lane. Then there's Bob.

Bob likes to swim his laps from the top corner of one side of the "L" to the bottom corner of the other side. He traverses the pool diagonally, taking up the entire pool. Bob doesn't know how to swim very well, so he splashes down his arms and legs in such a fashion as to create tsunami-like waves in the entire pool. Even when there are already others using the pool before Bob, he seems oblivious (or couldn't care less) and proceeds with his swim. Bob thinks the entire pool belongs to him, and he does not know how to stay in his lane.

These two examples typify people who like to be in control. However if we all are honest, relinquishing control is a scary prospect for most of us. If I am totally honest with myself, there are things in my life that I do to be in control, but I might call it being organized or "on top of things." Let's face it — chaos is frightening, so we do our best to keep everything in our lives under our control. This is rather humorous when one considers that we are spinning through space on a ball of dirt over which we have zero control. In reality, considering the greatness of the universe, how much control do we think we could possibly have?

Our Heavenly Father and Creator of all is actually the One who *does* have control. All of creation originated from Him, and because of His omniscience, omnipotence and omnipresence, He knows exactly what is best. In His love and concern for us, He asks that we would trust Him with our lives. In order to do that, we must surrender our will to His will and give Him control. The good news is that with each level of sweet surrender we achieve, there awaits profound peace and joy, and a life with ultimate fulfillment: "Remember, your Father knows exactly what you need even before you ask him!" Matthew 6:8 (TLB)

Whispers of the Divine

You perceive that My desire to have control over your life is invasive. All experience with the fallen nature suffers from an independent spirit, and yours is compounded with having been raised in a society where total independence and self-sufficiency are highly valued. You don't want to draw close to Me because you are afraid that then you won't be able to do whatever it is that you want to do. Pride and rebellion are at the root. You must make a decision to allow Me to deliver you from this. You mistakenly think that I want control in order to deprive you of what you want. Nothing could be further from the truth. Your yielding to Me will actually be the most fulfilling path for your life. Your expectation of a happy life is not My certainty of what will truly satisfy and fulfill you. I did not say that your life will be without conflict, trials, troubles or difficulty — but that is what you think it must be like for you to be happy. You will learn that trials can lead to treasures of wisdom and knowledge. Conflict can forge stronger relationships. Trouble can cultivate an attitude of gratitude, and difficulties can be the breeding ground for success. My thoughts are above your thoughts, and My ways are above your ways. All that I ask is that you trust Me and have faith in Me — I will do the rest. The more you resist, the farther you go from what you really desire.

Read My Word, and meditate upon Me. You have heard Me say to the Pharisees that they would search the scriptures in hopes of finding Me, but they did not find Me. They found their interpretation of scripture. I am a person to be known by the heart, not by the head. You can know about Me, and yet not know Me. This is something you must practice because it does not come natural to you. I will help you, but you must sit quietly and just be. Resist the temptation to do. I know this is difficult for you, but I will help you. You will find that after awhile it will be easy and natural for you to let go and just be.

You don't like doing that because you feel out of control, but that's ok because I take pleasure in being in control. Think of it as floating in a gentle current. When you fight the current it is a struggle, but when you relax and allow the current to uphold you and carry you, then you have a wonderful ride. My Spirit will take you on a wonderful ride. Relax, enjoy! Out of your innermost being will flow rivers of living water.

Lay it down. Lay it all down. Lay it down, and stop carrying it. Let it all go, and release it to me. Did I not save you when you didn't even know the need was there? Have I not ordained all the days of your life before you were even born? Was it not I who gave you the gifts and talents that you possess? I am the One who has planned your life out for you even as I uphold the plan of the universe and all creatures great and small. Read Matthew 6 again with a deliberate open heart to allow the Holy Spirit to transform you by My Word. It would also be helpful to express thanksgiving often. Thanksgiving shows that you understand that I am responsible for your life, *not you. Being thankful helps you to realize that life is a gift. Just as you have no control over any gift that is given to you freely, you must understand that the gift of life that I have given to you comes freely and without effort on your part. And, don't be so serious all the time —take time to do things that you enjoy —explore a little. You need to learn how to have fun!*

Chapter Four

FAITH

Faith doesn't remain status quo. It will grow, or it will go.
—Unknown

It's Not Like The Blind Leading the Blind

Stepping out in faith can lead to an extraordinary adventure with God. I remember distinctly a time in my life when I made such a choice. I was living in Northern California at the time, in a lovely home with my two children —a girl, 16 years of age; a boy 12 years of age. My spouse of almost 20 years had just made a decision to end our marriage, and so he had left to live elsewhere without us. Needless to say, it was an extremely distressing time for all of us.

I was trying to decide what to do next, since my home had gone into foreclosure, and I was about to lose everything. Through a sequence of events over the course of a few months after testing the waters in several possible directions, I decided to pack up and move to Tulsa, Oklahoma, to attend Bible college. It seemed like a radical decision, but I sensed this was the right move.

I had never been to Oklahoma, and I didn't know anyone there. I didn't have a job, and I didn't even know if I had been accepted into the Bible college yet. However, I had taken a quick trip to Tulsa previously to see if I could find a place for my children and I to live. Through a dramatic series of events, God led me to the exact right place — a two-story, three-bedroom duplex. I hired a driver to take us from California to Oklahoma in a forty foot Penske truck, with my car on a trailer behind us. When we arrived, my daughter and I were greeted by the unfamiliar, suffocating, Midwest August heat and humidity as we unloaded our belongings.

Drenched in sweat, exhausted and drained from the travel and moving, I distinctly remember sitting on the landing upstairs after everything was in our new rental home in Tulsa. I was shocked to hear a voice so loud and distinct (I was certain it was audible) say, Thank you. It was the voice of Father God thanking me for being obedient, for trusting Him, and for moving in faith. I was brought to tears to think that the God of the universe would thank me for anything!

As it turned out, my six years in Tulsa became a six-year journey in faith. Every time I needed money for tuition, food, or other resources, it was always provided. I also made many good friends while I was there, and stay in touch with some of them to this day. After I graduated from Bible college, God created a custom-made position for me not previously in existence to teach the third-year mission students. He also miraculously provided two other jobs; teaching at a community college, and working as a librarian in an elementary school.

I could not possibly recount all of the amazing events that transpired in those six years that I spent in Tulsa, but they were all God-orchestrated. It was a season of profound healing for me. I was brought back to my true identity and purpose. I grew in faith and my knowledge of the Word of God. More importantly, I grew to know Him more intimately. All of this and more began with that first step of faith.

Whispers of the Divine

I would like you to have faith in My love for you. Perfect love casts out all fear. As you trust in My love for you, you will be released from all the fear the enemy has had you in all your lifetime. As you saw recently, fear is the foothold the enemy uses to gain entrance to your life. When you are free from fear, he has no effective strategy against you. When you are full of love, faith and righteousness, his strategies are completely ineffective. Trust in My love, lean into My love — not in a general sense, but in a very specific and ongoing moment-by-moment way. When you sense your reaction is one of fear, concern, or anxiety, cast it upon Me and lean into My love. Attend to the power of My love at that precise moment to deliver you from fear. Fear is also the sin that so easily besets you. It may come in various forms, but it is the same basic absence of the consciousness of My love. Develop your faith in My love. Worship Me, and you will find yourself in the Presence of My love. The deeper your worship of Me, the deeper you will go into My love.

In your heart you do believe, and you do trust, but you are distracted by circumstances. My Word is truth. Faith comes by hearing and hearing by My word, My voice to you. What are you hearing right now? Do not allow the circumstances to unnerve you. Do not allow the distractions to cause your gaze to move away from Me. Do not allow the many voices in the world, in your head, in your circumstances to distract you from the voice of peace that I bring to you. What are you hearing right now? Listen to what is going on inside of you and move toward Me. Move into the light, move into the peace, move into the freedom, move into the river of life, move to the banqueting table that I have prepared for you before your enemies. Refuse to partake of what the enemy offers. REFUSE it! Partake of righteousness, peace and joy, which is My kingdom. You can turn to the monster, or you can turn to the Master. Turn to Me, My love!

Chapter Five

FATHER'S WILL

Happiness is only attained by the free will agreeing in its freedom to accord with the will of God.
—Sabine Baring-Gould

Father Knows Best

As an aspiring wordsmith, I enjoy reading, writing and studying languages, including my native tongue — the English language. There are so many fascinating aspects to language, such as the parts of speech and their function. I like to play with words, such as the use of alliteration or onomatopoeia. Prefixes are fun because they change the meaning of a word. The prefix *re-* is particularly exciting to me. There are so many amazing words with that particular prefix which I think reveal the precious will of our Heavenly Father.

God's original plan was to create a speaking spirit made in His image and likeness with whom He could have relationship and fellowship. The crowning glory of all His creation was mankind. He made them male and female and walked and talked with them in the cool of the day. Unfortunately, one particular day changed the course of history for all humanity. It was that fateful moment in the Garden of Eden when Adam and Eve *rebelled* against God the Creator by eating the fruit of the tree of the knowledge of good and evil. The consequence was banishment from God's Presence and death to their spiritual connection.

Not only did the couple violate the Father's will, they also forfeited their God-given authority to the archenemy, fallen Lucifer. As a Father, God was not satisfied to be separated from His children, and so He devised a plan to *restore* mankind into His family again on a permanent basis — never more to be estranged. His original plan became His eternal plan.

An essential part of His perfect plan was to send His Son, Jesus, in order to *re*deem mankind from the clutches of His enemy by paying the *redemption* price and taking the punishment for man's sin. Because of the power of the *resurrection*, any person who accepts this tremendous gift can be spiritually *regenerated* by the Holy Spirit into *renewed* relationship with the Father. Once again His children are *reconnected* to God the Father. Not only that, but they receive a ministry to *reconcile* others to the Father. Mankind can return to God's original design.

The grace and the Presence of God the Father *repositions* us in His will, *refreshes* us with His Spirit, and *reaffirms* and *reestablishes* our sonship. Under the headship of Christ, we are *reinstated* to our position of authority on earth. Now, isn't all that *remarkable*! Feel free to *re-read* this!

Whispers of the Divine

It is essential that you know the will of the Father. Without your mind set on His will, it is impossible to crucify the flesh. Only when you can see the brilliance of His plan and purpose, can your mind be willing to direct your flesh. This takes revelation. Paul knew this, and that is why I had him fashion the prayers in Ephesians. Knowing the heart of the Father and having His will in focus is of utmost importance. Ask the Father to show you His will in every situation.

It is, after all, My Father's intention for all to be transformed into My image, even as I am a perfect reflection of His image. Don't parents delight in seeing the reflection of themselves in their children? These verses in the Pauline prayers of the first and third chapters of Ephesians show Paul's dogged determination and commitment to seeing the will of the Father perfected in those he ministered to. Again, you must have revelation of the will of the Father in order to set your mind toward His plan and purpose at any cost.

Be authentic and genuine at all times. Do not be hypocritical or have pretense about anything. Be genuine and true to yourself, to Me, and to others. The more you accurately see yourself in My Word as My Son Jesus did, the more fully you will complete My will for your life. He saw Himself in the Scriptures, and was able to fulfill His mission on earth. He never tried to be or do anything outside of who He knew He was. This is a good example to follow. I will help you with this through My Spirit, but you must seek it.

Chapter Six

FORGIVENESS

The weak can never forgive. Forgiveness is the attribute of the strong.
—Mahatma Gandhi

A Sweet Aroma?

Forgiveness is a big deal to God. His entire plan of salvation and the dedication of Christ's life on earth were all about forgiveness. There existed only one entrance into renewed relationship with our Heavenly Father, and that was based upon the fact that He was willing to forgive every single person of every single sin, offense, or debt, regardless of how big or small. Consequently, if we are not willing to forgive someone who has, in some way, done us wrong, God is very clear about His response. He simply will not forgive us if we refuse to forgive others. Ouch!

Our unwillingness to forgive others is so egregious and abhorrent to God that it is a stench in His nostrils. The Bible is clear that our thoughts and words are powerful — for life or death. However, did you know that these expressions have such an impact in the spiritual world that they also emit an aroma or odor? Depending on the quality of thoughts and words we are releasing into the atmosphere, they can be pleasant or they can stink.

Think of the sweet fragrance of a lovely flower. That is the sort of aroma that attracts bees and hummingbirds and humans. By contrast, imagine the stench of a rotting carcass. That smell of death attracts vultures and other such scavengers. Our life-giving thoughts and words attract the heavenly spiritual realm. On the other hand, our negative thoughts and words attract the dark side of the spiritual realm. Harboring unforgiveness in our hearts is one sure way of permeating our thoughts, words and actions with a distinctively unpleasant smell — one that reeks to high heaven.

The sweet fragrance of Christ is the aroma of forgiveness, and it is one that is pleasing to the Father.

Forgiveness is the greatest gift and the richest treasure that has been given to us by God, and it is the most powerful thing that we could ever release to someone else. The act of forgiving impacts the giver as much as the one being forgiven. It is as though one walks out of a dark cave through a flood of cascading and cleansing water into the light of day. We forgive because we are forgiven, and the powerful, waterfall of forgiveness covers every wrong — past, present and future — because of the cleansing flood of the Blood of Jesus.

> 15 For we are the sweet fragrance of Christ [which ascends] to God, [discernible both] among those who are being saved and among those who are perishing; 16 to the latter one an aroma from death to death [a fatal, offensive odor], but to the other an aroma from life to life [a vital fragrance, living and fresh].
>
> 2 Corinthians 2:15-16 (AMP)

Whispers of the Divine

You know how to forgive, but you need to learn how to release. When you release a situation into My care, then I am able to carry that care and take care of it. Until you truly release the situation, you are yourself carrying it. That is what brings the negative to pass. Allow Me to get involved by prayer and a determination to hand things over to Me. I know how to work in the hearts of men. You must release as well as forgive. If you want the situation to change, you must allow Me to work in that person's life. Expect a different outcome when the Holy Spirit becomes active in the circumstance.

This will give you hope instead of despair. It will build your faith for things to be different. If you have a negative expectation, then you cannot have a positive outcome. Hope in Me. I am well able.

Chapter Seven

FREE WILL

Day by day, what you choose, what you think and what you do
is who you become.
—Heraclitus

Your Secret Power

Are you a superhero? Do you have a super power? Well, one can dream! Actually, we as human beings have been given a secret power that is super powerful! The most valuable gift we have ever received from our Creator is that of personal sovereignty — our ability to choose what to think and to believe for ourselves. We have the gift of free will. This tremendous right is what distinguishes each individual from every other person and from all the rest of creation.

We don't always have control over our circumstances, nor do we have control over the choices that other people make. Sometimes we'd like to, but that's the thing about free will — if we exert our will to control someone else, then we are taking away their ability to choose for themselves.

Even in the most extreme of circumstances, when individuals are imprisoned or held captive by enemy forces, even then, deep on the inside they can choose what to think or believe. We can resist the temptation to give in to fear, negativity, or discouragement simply by choosing to think differently — to believe for something better, to hope instead of despair. The stories of people who have done this over the centuries even in dire situations are plentiful and inspiring.

If we go back to the book of Genesis, we see that when God designed mankind, He desired to create a being in His own image and likeness. He made them male and female, and gave them dominion over all the facets of creation on the earth. God is love, and Love gave His human beings the ability to choose to love Him in return — or not. His precious children could choose to spend all eternity with their Heavenly Father, or apart from Him. This is the risk He was willing to take. Even Almighty God will not violate the precious gift and grace He has endowed on His creation. Is it not best, then, to yield to the good will of God for our lives here on earth and hereafter in eternity?

Whispers of the Divine

When your position was taken away, you felt like you were not able to make choices for your own life. You became angry that their decision so negatively impacted your life on many levels (or so you thought). You do have the gift of free will, but it is limited to certain choices in your life. When it comes to decisions that other people make which can affect your life, you do not have a choice in those matters. Many people find this to be the point of contention and strife when two wills collide with each other. This is where submission comes in. This is where love comes in. I have told you to submit yourselves in love to one another. Love will always win and never fail. But trying to get your way all the time will only lead to heartbreak. I submitted My will to the Father because He is great and good and knows best. His plan was executed in love and required submission to complete. Whenever human will runs antagonistic to God the Father's will, the only intelligent choice is to submit and do things His way, for His way is perfect.

Chapter Eight

FREEDOM

For to be free is not merely to cast off one's chains, but to live in a way that respects and enhances the freedom of others.
—Nelson Mandela

Grace or Disgrace?

When you hear the word *sin*, what comes to mind? When the topic of sin is approached, it often makes us feel uncomfortable, perhaps because we perceive that this is God's attempt to have an excuse to punish us, or to deprive us of all the fun in life. Then again, maybe it is that we feel our own guilt in failing to be our best selves.

When you hear the word, *grace*, what comes to mind? What is the relationship of grace to sin? Is it like God's Get-out-of-jail-free card as in the game Monopoly? Grace is so all encompassing and such an integral part of our spiritual lives that it is spiritually to us what physically breathing air is for us. Grace is the empowering Presence of God freely given to us, enabling us to be who He has created us to be, and to do what He has called us to do. We daily desperately need His grace!

Proverbs 18:3 says: "Sin brings disgrace." When we break down the word, *dis-grace* we can see the prefix *dis*, meaning separation, negation, reversal or deprived of. *Grace* is the unmerited favor and love of God toward mankind, and His divine influence acting beneficently upon mankind. Why would we want to intentionally separate ourselves from the power of God, which is actually for our benefit?

Our good Father knows that sin brings pain and suffering to His children. Think of the anguish, hurt and human destruction that come from lies, cheating, divorce, theft, addictions, violence, murder, rejection, abuse, rage and an endless list of the violations of God's love. We live in a corrupted world, and this is why we need a perpetual supply of the powerful grace of God.

He has forever removed the disconnect that dis-grace brought us, and has instead reconnected us to His lavish grace. When we realize that God has once and for all dealt with the sin issue by having punished the Man Christ Jesus, and by having laid all the blame and wrath upon Him for our sin, then we can be free to endlessly avail ourselves of His grace, and experience delicious freedom from the bondage and disgrace of sin.

Whispers of the Divine

Thank you for letting me remove these burdens from your heart. Thank you for releasing them to Me. I want nothing more than for you to be free. It is why I came. You must think differently to be different. When you let go of all the mindsets that keep you weighed down, then you can buoy up into a life of faith and hope and love. I never designed for you to be weighed down by sin or worries. These are the things I spoke of in the book of Hebrews that you are to cast off and lay aside so that you can run the course. Run, My little one, run like the wind, run with the horses. You can do it! You are free in Me. You are empowered by My Holy Spirit — the All Powerful One. There is nothing that you cannot do with Me. I am your strength, your hope, your song. Sing, My little one. Sing to Me the song of freedom. Let your heart soar with joy, the joy of your salvation. I have come to set you free!

Freedom. My vision for the entire world is freedom. I have come to set all free. In your nation, the theme of freedom has been distorted to mean self-serving. But I have spoken in My Word that freedom means your life of service can now be to Me and no longer need be a life of slavery to the evil one. The climate of heaven and the standard of My kingdom is to serve others. The more you do that here on the earth, the more you will replicate the atmosphere of heaven here. I desire for all people to discover their individual identities, and to use the gifts and talents I have given them to serve the world.

Individual by individual, city by city, state by state, and country by country — bringing My kingdom to earth as it is in heaven.

My utmost desire for you is freedom! I desire your spiritual freedom from the chains of sin and failure and the things of darkness that have captivated and kept you in bondage. Freedom in relationships — first of all with Me and then with yourself and others. I desire freedom from physical pain, disease, sickness and limitations. I want you free emotionally from all the experiences that have crippled you and made you less than I created you to be. Financial freedom, intellectual freedom — freedom, total and complete for the whole being. It is for freedom that I have set you free. Where the Spirit of the Lord is, there is freedom. Pursue freedom for yourself and others, and you will be in agreement with Me.

I have designed you to be free and fulfilled. It is natural for you to be frustrated when you do not live in the completeness of freedom or of fulfillment. But the truth is, that I have also made you to be powerful. You can be strong in Me and in the power of My might. Use My Word to create the realities that you desire in your life, just as I used My word to create the realities I desired. You are not powerless; you are powerful. Allow yourself to dream with Me. I will show you the potential and the possibilities. These are not just nice sayings. I can show you the realities that I desire to create in your life. Dream with Me. Dreaming will give you hope, and hope will be the substance for your faith to be released. I am the God of all hope, and I want to fill your life with hope of all kinds. Dream with Me.

If all My people would just practice My Presence, it would solve all of their issues, problems and sins. The fullness of My Presence is all you or anyone else needs. I want you free! I long to see you fully liberated in the glory of my work on the cross! Breathe in My essence; allow my grace to saturate your days; take time to contemplate

Who I am and allow Me to show you more. How I long for you to know Me and to be complete in Me in your daily experience.

Chapter Nine

FULFILLMENT

The greatest wealth is to live content with little.
—Plato

Happy in Xalapa

Some of my greatest adventures in life have happened on the mission field. Numerous times these mission trips were to the country of Mexico. On one such trip I was living with a lovely national family in Mexico City. The husband was a prominent attorney in the country. He decided that he and his wife should take me on a trip to Vera Cruz to see where he had been born. They were very eager to share this experience with me, and insisted on paying for all the expenses of the trip.

It was a delightful experience, and wonderful to see an area of Mexico that I had never visited before. The cuisine that far south in Mexico was a delicious change from that in Mexico City. Every region in the country of Mexico has its own distinct expressions in art, architecture, music, food, landscape, and so on. The highlight of the trip for me happened when my host decided to visit some of his colleagues at a home in Xalapa, which is the capital of Vera Cruz.

We arrived in the late afternoon at a villa that was high up in the hills. As I walked through the front door, my eyes met with the most stunning view. The entire rear side of the house was open to the outside because the walls folded sideways in panels to allow the breeze to flow through. There was a large patio extension to the home with furniture, which included table and chairs set up for dinner. On one side of the patio was an infinity pool that appeared to cascade down the side of a lush, deep canyon. Beyond the canyon were the emerald colored hills on the other side. Overhead large birds were soaring — eagles, perhaps. It was so still and quiet that you could hear your own heart beating. The view literally took my breath away. It was exquisite!

I walked to the edge of the cliff to get a better view of the canyon. I just stood there taking it all in. Now, if ever I had doubted that God knew me better than I know myself, those doubts were put to rest in one moment of time. As I surveyed the spectacular scene, I heard a voice in my heart ask this question, You really like this, don't you? Somewhat surprised by the question, I answered, Yes, Lord, it is beautiful. Then I heard the voice again, swelling with joy and excitement. I knew you would! I have been waiting all your life just for this moment to show this to you!

That was it. I knew then, and have known since then that my Heavenly Father knows everything about me. He knows everything about you, too.

Whispers of the Divine

Happiness and fulfillment are two different things. You can feel happy and not be fulfilled, but you cannot be fulfilled and be unhappy. Fulfillment is the greatest joy because it lines up with My plans and purposes. Satisfaction and delight come when the intended purpose is complete or fulfilled. This is by My design. When you seek My way, you will have both joy and fulfillment. This is why I say to seek first the Kingdom of heaven and all these things will be added to you. In the Kingdom of heaven it is My plans and My purposes that are fulfilled. I am the Author of creation, so each and every thing and being that I have created has unique purpose. You must live in accordance with My will and destiny in order to find the fulfillment that you seek.

I want you to be fully satisfied with your life. I want you to be fulfilled, and filled with My life. My life is abundant and free. It is overflowing, ample, and in full measure for every area of your life. Physically, emotionally, provisionally, spiritually, socially — every need is amply supplied. I know you, and I have anticipated what it will take to fulfill your life.

Your task is to know Me. I AM light. I AM life. I AM that I AM. I encompass all things within and without. It is impossible to escape My Presence, for I am everywhere. But not all are aware of My Presence. You can help Me to be seen and known to others as you see Me and know Me yourself. Seek this, for in this is the fulfillment of all else.

Chapter Ten

HEALING

Heal me, O Lord, and I shall be healed; save me, and I shall be saved;
for you are my praise.
—Jeremiah 17:14

The Miracle Worker

The principal of one of the schools where I worked was an enthusiast about team building. Before classes began at the beginning of every school year she would have faculty and staff spend an entire week doing activities that involved teamwork. One particular year we were given an assignment to read a book about discovering our individual personal strengths. It was at this time I discovered that my greatest personal strength is empathy.

This discovery shed a lot of light on the reason behind the fact that one of my passions has always been to pray for people to be healed. I can't stand to see people suffer, and it just seemed logical to me that God doesn't like that either. He did send His Son to suffer and die for us, and when He walked on the earth He spent much of His time healing innumerable people.

I am not ignorant of the fact that the topic of healing is surrounded by much controversy. Nor do I pretend to have answers to the many questions that arise when people do not receive healing. I myself have had dear friends die even after much prayer. In spite of the perplexity of these experiences, I still firmly believe that it is possible to be healed.

Over the course of more than four decades, I have prayed for many people, and have seen some remarkable results. There was a young teen who was bowed over with scoliosis. But after prayer, she immediately stood up a full six inches taller with a straight spine. A little boy was virtually blind, and he began to see clearly after prayer. A woman came to me with complete adrenal shut down. She decided to come for prayer instead of going to the hospital right away. Instantaneously, she received new adrenals and was completely healed.

When my daughter was twelve years old, she had a friend who had to wear a back brace because of the severity of her scoliosis. As I prayed for her, she was healed. When she returned to her doctor, she was told she did not need any brace. Now she is 38 years old, married, and has had two children of her own. I could go on and on. I acknowledge that I don't know all that there is to know about the matter, but I have seen many healings and miracles.

I will continue to believe what the Bible says in both the Old and the New Testaments about the goodness of God to heal us, and I encourage you to open your heart to the power of His healing touch:

> But He was wounded for our transgressions, He was bruised for our iniquities; The chastisement for our peace was upon Him, And by His stripes we are healed.
>
> Isaiah 53:5

> Who Himself bore our sins in His own body on the tree, that we, having died to sins, might live for righteousness—by whose stripes you were healed.
>
> 1Peter 2:24

Whispers of the Divine

Always look to Me first and foremost. Strive to stay in tune with the flow of the Holy Spirit. There is a huge discrepancy between the natural realm and the spiritual realm. The spiritual realm is more powerful than the natural realm — by FAR. The more you can yield to My working in the spirit realm, the more effective you will be in healing. Never rely upon your own understanding, always lean on My wisdom and direction in every situation — even if is it is similar to a previous situation.

There are many factors involved in healing including the person who is receiving (or resisting) the healing, the people who are administering the healing, and the spiritual influences at work — either from My Kingdom or the kingdom of darkness. The only way to discern all of the elements that need to be addressed is to listen to the voice of the Holy Spirit. So, quiet yourself down, and breathe deeply of My Presence before you move forward. Listen attentively, be ready to move in whatever direction is given to you, and trust the outcome to Me.

I am always healing. I am always healing. There is unending power over all that is not righteous flowing from My being. Worship Me and the power will overtake you.

Chapter Eleven

IDENTITY

I would rather be what God chose to make me than the most glorious creature that I could think of; for to have been thought about, born in God's thought, and then made by God, is the dearest, grandest and most precious thing in all thinking.
—George MacDonald

Whose DNA?

Ice cream is one of my favorite foods, but not ice cream just by itself. It has to have crunch to it, so it needs to have nuts or something crunchy to contrast the smooth creaminess of this cold confection. Where did I come up with this preference? I think it must have been from my dad. Every night he would have a big bowl of ice cream and sprinkle Grape Nuts cereal on top. When he and I would go out for a special treat, it would be ice cream. As good Catholics, for Lent my dad and I used to give up ice cream. As soon as the 40 days of Lent were over the night before Easter, we would go to midnight Mass. Immediately afterwards we'd go to the nearest 24-hour diner and get a big banana split — with nuts on top!

Even though my dad is no longer with us, and many decades have passed since I lived in his home, his influence lives on in me. What I look like and who I am in the natural is a blend of nature (the inherited traits from my parents) and nurture (the learned behaviors from their training). When I look at my parents, I identify with some of their physical traits and some of their behaviors, and consequently begin to learn who I am.

However, I don't just have a natural life, I also am a spiritual being. According to the Bible, once I received life from God the Father, through Jesus Christ by the Holy Spirit, I became a brand new creation — a new species of being. Since I have been fathered from above, I now have inherited a new spiritual DNA, and I can be newly trained in behaviors befitting a heavenly Kingdom. I have a new identity.

Whispers of the Divine

You are first and foremost, My child. I love you with an everlasting love. I have chosen you for Myself- to go where I go and to do what I do. Your identity is to be like Me — gracious, kind and loving. Beyond that, I have given you certain gifts to help others. You have allowed your identity to fall into the hands of others, but now I am recovering that for you. Never allow others to tell you who you are –always go to My Word and see yourself there. That is what I did to find Myself in the scriptures when I conversed with the Father. Who you are is so much more than what you do. Your identity is never only one thing for one time. It is who you are in every moment as you draw life from Me. Therefore, who you are is who you allow Me to be in you. Never see yourself apart from or independent of Me. I am the Vine and you are the branch. You think that if you're not thinking about Me that I am not with you — but intuitively you are receiving of My life, My love, My thoughts.

It is very important that you understand son-ship. Why do you think that I took the time to include the lineage and information about who was whose son? It denotes belonging and identity. You will never fulfill your destiny without knowing your identity. It is I who give you your identity. I have given you the right to be a son of God. This is who you are. This is who you will be forever.

This is why you must know Me as the Son of God, so you will receive your destiny as sons of God. Read what the Gospels say about Me and how I lived as the Son of God, and you will see how you should live. This may sound simple and obvious, but few of my children actually live out of their sonship. Seek to please Me as a child seeks to please his or her father. Imitate Me in all that you see Me say and do. This was the example that I left for you. Identify with Me in My nature as I identified with you in your human nature. You cannot successfully do this without spending much time with Me and in My Word. That has to be a priority in your life. The basics are the most true and valuable for success.

If you could see Me in all my glory, you would know that I can outshine all of your darkness, overpower all of your weakness, right all of your wrongs, and vastly contribute to any lack of resources you may have. This is why I am always encouraging my children to see Me for Who I AM. However, most of my children see themselves for who they are not. Come close to Me, let Me shine on you with My glory.

Remember that I am utterly and completely human, but I am also fully God Almighty. When I came to earth to occupy a human body, it was for the purpose of forever changing the fate of the human race. When I come into your humanity to dwell within your heart, it is to forever change your identity and destiny. I long for my people to see beyond the natural into the glorious life of the spirit. Many do, but not with the consistency that would keep them moving forward at the rate of growth I would have for them. There is much to do on the earth before I return, but so many are occupied with the cares of this world that it is difficult for them to see beyond their own needs, wants and problems. Let us move forward together. The more you allow Me to heal you, the more free you will be to walk, run and even fly with Me. Set your mind on things above where you are seated with Me in heavenly places. This is what I ask of you today — not to look into the past, but look into your future.

All things were brought into existence by Me. All things are held together by Me and My word of power. I existed before all, and will always exist. There is nothing outside of Me either in the realm of space or time. I encompass all. If you view your life as a connection to Me and not as something that you live out apart from Me, then you will surely be blessed. The more that you can acknowledge Me in your existence, the more that My existence will fill you.

That would include My love (or better stated, My personhood because love is who I am). Constantly be tuned into who I am in you, around you, through you, and for you. The more connection you make with Me, the more you will know Me. You have no idea the level of intimacy I am capable of sharing with you. You desire intimacy — you desire to be known and appreciated and acknowledged as valuable. You are. I KNOW you because I made you. I appreciate you because you are My creation, and I acknowledge your value by giving all that I have in Christ Jesus for you.

My child, you are ever with Me in my abode of heaven. I have made a place for you. You have a home, and you have a family. I am your home, and I am your family. I am your own Father. There is never a moment that I am not thinking of you to bless you. I cover you with My wings, I surround you with my grace and compassion. You belong to Me. You have a place of belonging. Don't look at the circumstances of this world to determine your identity. Your identity is in Me - forevermore.

Remember the men on the road to Emmaus? They could not see who I was without Me opening their eyes. You have cultivated a life of independence — which is not good, but you are beginning to realize how valuable dependence upon Me is. That is good. You truly cannot do anything of spiritual consequence or value without Me, just as I knew that as a man (bereft of My Godly omnipotence, omniscience and omnipresence) I could do nothing apart from the Father. Let Me be your example in this — learn from Me. I am humble and gentle and meek. You have learned that it is important to be strong, and you have valued human strength, and even have idolized human achievement. But I tell you that when you are weak, then I am strong. That is the strength you should go after. Glory in your weakness because then you will abound in My strength.

Now, turn around from the way you have been, and you can begin a new path with Me.

You don't always have to be the teacher or counselor. Sometimes you just need to affirm people. Affirm them in who I made them to be — who they actually ARE in Me. Focus more on who they are and not what they do. When you look at people based on identity rather than behavior, you can be more encouraging to them, and this also brings their focus to the center of reality for themselves — who they are created to be. This always lifts people up, restores their hope and vision, and can activate their purpose. Besides, it will make you feel better about your interaction with them because you like to encourage and lift people up.

VISION:I see Jesus flying up into the sky in white robes that are shimmering with gold dust all over, and He leaves a trail of glittering gold in His wake. Then I am suddenly walking with him down a majestic hallway — like a classical colonnade - with huge white marble columns on both sides of a white marble floor. I am wearing a type of silky white gown or robe. It is so bright in this place– there is so much light! I look happy. I see huge volumes of books and I sense that the Lord is saying these contain the answers to all my questions. I open one, and glittering golden light streams out. I think I instantaneously received understanding and revelation about something that I didn't understand before. I sense that the Lord is saying that whenever I have a question about something that I can come with Him into this room to find the answers that I need. I am thinking of the scripture that says that Jesus is made to me to be a treasury of wisdom and understanding. This is pretty remarkable because I have always craved to understand things, and it really troubles me to not understand something. This is an amazing gift from the Lord!

Chapter Twelve

INTENTIONALITY

No! Try not! Do or do not. There is no try.
—Yoda

Try Not

Several years ago I was teaching at a Christian school in Pacific Palisades, California. One of my students was also the daughter of a colleague who was the second grade teacher. Her daughter had been diagnosed with Leukemia when she was very young. After much prayer and some treatment, she became cancer free. Every year she and her mom made a pilgrimage to the hospital on the East Coast where she had been treated in order to encourage the other children there who were still battling cancer.

One particular year, mom and daughter were commemorating her 10-year anniversary of freedom from Leukemia, and all the school was celebrating her victory. I was so impressed with her mother who was very involved with the organization called Team in Training, which sponsors various events to raise money for the Leukemia and Lymphoma Society. I admired the fact that she was frequently doing a marathon or triathlon, and was in excellent physical shape.

One day, as we passed in the hallway, I mentioned my admiration for her and her dedication to doing these events. In response, she simply said, "You could do it." I don't know why, but these few words penetrated deep inside me and ignited a desire to accomplish a physical challenge beyond anything I had ever done. So at 62 years of age, I signed up to run a half marathon with Team in Training.

The great thing about this organization is that they have a very specific plan. Their coaches have a lot of experience in training people through all facets of preparation — from choosing the right shoes and gear for running, to fundraising, and everything in between. So, beginning in mid-October through mid-January, I trained with them. However, I was far from perfect during training and sometimes made excuses why I couldn't run or follow the eating plan.

Here are some of the discoveries I made on the day of the marathon: Being intentional about completing a goal is paramount. The discipline of day-by-day choices is critical to a good outcome. Being a whiney-baby when something encroaches on my comfort zone is not productive. I can make my body do things it doesn't want to do, even when it screams at me, if I am intentional and focused on the finish line. Listen to the coaches — they know how to follow the plan and win the race.

I did make it across the finish line, received the medal, and now have the status of being an "elite" athlete. Plus, I raised about $2600.00 for the charity. All of this because I heard four words, "You could do it."

God has a plan. A plan is a vehicle through which a purpose comes into being. We need God's plan to fulfill God's purpose in our lives. We can become the embodiment of the plan of God by aligning our wills with the Almighty. Do you know His plan for you?

Whispers of the Divine

My Father is a planner. He never does anything without a plan. You should set the course of your life by setting your heart each day. It is like a compass, like setting the sails to catch the wind to go in a particular direction. You must decide to see, and do, and live in the Spirit each day, and throughout the day. Keep adjusting your course to the inner compass of your heart. Set your heart upon Me. Set your heart upon My Kingdom. Set your heart upon the Spirit life within you. Be deliberate as you go through your day. Many of My people are caught up in the natural flow of events each day, and consequently feel helpless, but this does not have to be the way. There is a power source within you, available to you at every moment of every day and night. He is the great Spirit Who is ready and available to breathe upon your heart and mind, and even enliven your mortal body when asked to do so. You must be conscious and aware that in Me you live and move and have your being. Act like it is so, because it is. My people live far below their privileges much of the time, and labor and are burdened by the circumstances of life. This is not My will. I have obtained all for them — victory, peace, unity, pardon, freedom, power, and it is My will that they live in all the honor and glory that I have given them. You can be an example to others as David was an example to My people. Let your life be an example of planning, purpose, and pursuit of Me. And praise Me. You will be happy you did.

All of my plans from eternity past, all of my purposes shall be culminated in Jesus. He is the One who has enabled Me to fulfill my pursuit of the human race to return to the close and intimate relationship that I have always desired with My people. All will know Me and My glory because of the One who came to show My glory. He put Me on display for the world to see. Even though all of nature displays my handiwork, it was Jesus who displayed My heart.

Chapter Thirteen

JOY

Joy is the infallible sign of the presence of God.
—Pierre Teilhard de Chardin

Thoughts That Spark Joy

What is it that brings you joy? Notice that I didn't ask, What makes you happy? because happiness and joy are two completely different things. Happiness is usually connected to what is happening, but joy can fill our hearts in spite of circumstances. When I am obedient or do something to please the Holy Spirit, I can feel His joy within me. This is the JOY that the Father has promised to me. It is the joy of God. His joy in me leads to my praise flowing out to Him.

Many years ago I challenged myself to write down what my life would look like if I were continuously filled with joy. As I recently reread the list of numerous items, it actually brought joy to my heart to think of what I could be doing by being a joy-filled person. They were things like:

- ◆ I would dance with abandon.
- ◆ I would glow and sparkle and walk with a spring in my step.
- ◆ I would look into the faces of people without shame or inferiority, and exude confidence and love.
- ◆ I would be creative and write, draw, paint, crochet, sew, craft, design, invent and produce things for the benefit of mankind.
- ◆ I would take time to soak in the amazing and immense beauty of people and creation.
- ◆ I would smile, laugh, and talk to strangers about God's love.
- ◆ I would sing all the time — even if I don't have perfect pitch.

- I would travel to many places and love many people.
- I would give away lots and lots — in big ways and small ways — just to see joy on the faces of others.
- I would be strong, healthy, and physically active.
- I would be still, peaceful, quiet and drink from the wells of salvation and rivers of life in Him.

I could go on with the list, but you get the idea. I'd like to challenge you to make your own Joy List, and then put it some place where you could look at it often. It will expand your vision and lift your spirits!

Whispers of the Divine

I will teach you what enjoyment in the Spirit is, so that you will find fulfillment in that and not have to cater to the indulgences of the flesh. Learn to distinguish the two. It is all about the motivation, the leaning of the heart, the setting of the affections. When your motivation is toward pleasing Me, your heart is leaning toward Me, and you have set your affections on Me and not self-love, then you will find pure joy — free from guilt and shame. But when you mind is set on meeting your own needs or desires, you will come up short because your resources are limited, and your joy will be oh so very fleeting. Worldly joy is transitory, but My joy abides forever in your heart. The more you please Me, the more joy you will have.

Chapter Fourteen

KINDNESS

Love and kindness are never wasted. They always make a difference. They bless the one who receives them, and they bless you, the giver.
— Barbara De Angelis

Random Acts of Kindness

When my daughter was young, one of her daily routines was to watch the program, *Mr. Rogers' Neighborhood*. She would sit captivated by the sound of his voice talking to her as if he were right there in the room with her. I have to admit, since I am an educator, I also enjoyed listening in to his programs and benefiting from his expert dealings with children. Mr. Rogers was not afraid to deal with difficult topics and current events that may be confusing to young minds. He was always there for them, and he was always absolutely kind.

Mr. Rogers didn't just exemplify kindness on his television show. He lived by showing kindness in his personal life. Many people don't realize the extent he went to in order to help children and others who were in need. He continually exuded kindness, and the world is a better place for it. We see this in some of his famous quotes like," "Imagine what our real neighborhoods would be like if each of us offered, as a matter of course, just one kind word to another person," and "There are three ways to ultimate success. The first way is to be kind. The second way is to be kind. The third way is to be kind."

I have been privileged to know many people over the course of my lifetime who stood out to me because of the quality of their kindness. When I was struggling through Bible College, the dean of the college was especially kind to me on many occasions. A dear friend who recently passed on to his eternal home exemplified kindness in all of his relationships. At his memorial, there was story after story told about how kind a person he was. It was a joy to be in his circle of influence.

Not long ago I decided to focus on the attribute of kindness, and for thirty days I explored various quotes from people dealing with the topic. It was a worthwhile pursuit. Kindness is powerful. Kindness has the power to bring encouragement to the weary and distressed. Kindness is able to diffuse volatile situations. Kindness can connect people who are otherwise strangers. The power of kindness has no limits to the influence it has on the myriad of human interactions.

Whispers of the Divine

I am kind. I will never think ill of you in any way, regardless of your behavior. I see you in the light of My glory, in perfection. I would never deny you anything that you desire within My will for your life. I am kind. I am giving because kindness gives freely without reproach. I cannot be diminished in who I am regardless of how much I give away of Myself. Reach for Me, expect Me to reach back to you and to embrace you as you desire to embrace Me. I will never desert you or leave you forsaken. It is my dearest desire to be with you always. We are one, you and I. Explore the depths of My being in your quiet times with Me. I have much to show you.

Chapter Fifteen

KINGDOM LIFE

The kingdom, Jesus taught, is right here – present yet hidden,
immanent yet transcendent. It is at hand – among us…
—Rachel Held Evans

The Kingdom Within

Imagine this scenario: You have spent the last few years of your life with a man who has turned your world upside down. He has spoken things that you have never heard before. He has demonstrated power beyond all human capability. Most importantly, he has lived a life of love never before experienced by the human heart. And then, he is forcibly taken from you, brutally beaten and suffers an unspeakably horrific death. You are crushed, your dreams are dashed to pieces, and you are terrified that your association with him means that you are next on the list. You have spent a few days hiding out with several others who had walked closely with this man when, suddenly, *He is back from the dead*!

Talk about a tumult of emotions! He tells you that He is a king — but not just any king. He is The King of all kings, and He has *all* authority on earth, in heaven and hell. He has the right to use *all* might, and then He tells you that He wants to give you the keys of His Kingdom. He gives *you* the right to use might in His Kingdom. So now suddenly you are the citizen of a different kingdom, with a different sovereign, where a different language is spoken, and you have been given power to exercise His will in the world to change the wrong to right. That's quite a paradigm shift, to say the least.

This scenario that we have just imagined is real. It is so real, that it supersedes all other realities. There are some words used in this account that we should examine to get the full impact of the truth of Kingdom Life. The first word I would like to address regarding the concepts of authority and power is *koach*, from the Hebrew word כּוֹחַ which means: strength, vigor, force, capacity, power, wealth, means, substance, and ability. The second word is ἐξουσία (*exousia*) from the Biblical Greek, which means: authority or right to act, ability, privilege, capacity, and delegated authority. The last word we need to look at is another Greek word: δύναμις (*dunamis*)which means energy, power, might, great force, great ability and strength. Christ has given us the right — *exousia* — to use His might — *dunamis.*

So Jesus arose from the dead, having been released from hell by the explosive power of the Holy Spirit, Who regenerated every cell in His human body — not just to a mortal state, but to an immortal state of being. He then told His followers that it was the good pleasure of Father God to give them the keys to the Kingdom, imagine what He was saying! This is what He is still saying to those of us who will follow Him. We can open our hearts and invite Him to reign and rule in His regency so that we may reach the world with a Kingdom of Love:

> For the kingdom of God is not eating and drinking, but righteousness and peace and joy in the Holy Spirit.
>
> Romans 14:17

> For the kingdom of God is not based on talk but on power.
>
> 1 Corinthians 4:20 (AMP)

> And Jesus summoned to Him His twelve disciples and gave them power and authority over unclean spirits, to drive them out, and to cure all kinds of disease and all kinds of weakness and infirmity.
>
> Matthew 10:1 (AMPC)

Whispers of the Divine

Come to Me freely and come to Me often. I have made the way for you. I have given the invitation to you. You should not fear. It is my Father's good pleasure to give you the keys of the Kingdom. It has always been Our design for you to rule and reign with Us. But just as a king goes through a season of preparation, my people must be prepared to rule and reign. That is what this season on earth is about. It is a time for learning how to enforce the victory, how to enlarge the Kingdom of God on earth as it is in heaven. As Romans 5:17 states, you will learn to reign in this life through Me. Come to Me, learn of Me. Most of My children have not yet learned to properly govern their own lives by My Word, much less subdue kingdoms. That is why I bid you to come to Me. Come to Me freely, come to Me often, learn of Me.

What you should be doing today is what you should be doing every day — take the time to become aware of My Kingdom that is within you and which surrounds you. You live in an alternate Kingdom. It is a supernatural Kingdom. The air you breathe in the Kingdom is rarified with My essence — My love. The Spirit permeates the atmosphere with vibrating, pulsating life. Thoughts become realities just by their inception. Music fills the air (so to speak) because it is an atmosphere like none other. Desires are instantly fulfilled. Your perspective should always and everyday be where you are seated with Me in heavenly places. Only then are you prepared to go down into the valley of earth to perform My will. But you will do so with power and Presence because of the time you have spent with Me. You will find the answers to your questions in the waiting on Me. There is a time to reveal all things, but not without the proper preparation, otherwise you could go ahead of My timing.

Come with Me. Let Me lead you on adventures that I have planned for you since the beginning of time. We will walk together, arm in arm, bringing light and life to a sick, dark and dying world. You will see how powerful My Kingdom is because it is able to overtake and overcome the strongest fortress of the enemy. All must bow before My Kingdom because I am the King over all kings and the Lord over all lords. My Kingdom is everlasting and can never be shaken — unlike other kingdoms, which are temporary and perishable.

Chapter Sixteen

LAW VS LOVE

The love of God is so rich it leaves our hearts full of heaven.
— Dr. Brian Simmons

The Sign Says, 'Do Not Pick the Flowers'!

One day as I was walking my dog, I came upon a woman who was violating our HOA rules by cutting the roses at the entrance to our clubhouse. My mind immediately judged her by the law of she should not be cutting our roses. Then, it was like a switch was turned on in my brain by the Holy Spirit to show me who she was — not just what she was doing.

He told me that she is a woman who loves flowers and the beauty of them and also desires to treasure that. Perhaps she is alone and is never given cut flowers, and just longs to have them in her home to bring her pleasure. He could feel her longing and her sense of guilt over having been caught doing something that should bring her joy.

This insight that He gave me immediately and completely changed my critical attitude toward someone I had never even met. I was overwhelmed not only by the love of God for me to show me how to be free from judging, but I was overwhelmed by His love for her! This profoundly touched my heart, and I was moved to tears.

It seems to me that love is the ultimate expression of intimacy. It is possible to know others, but without love that knowledge leads us to judge, criticize and tear down instead of accept, strengthen, encourage and comfort each other with faith. Because God is love, it appears that He has the deepest knowledge of each one of us. He knows every hidden thought and intention of our hearts.

Whispers of the Divine

It's not that there are no laws, it's that the laws should never supersede the love. The love is what governs life, not the laws. You think that I hold you to the laws, but I hold you to the law of LOVE. Laws are external, but love is internal. When you hold people to only what they should "do," you are not allowing them to "be." It is who they are that should matter to you, not what they do.

Chapter Seventeen

LEADERSHIP

If your actions inspire others to dream more, learn more, do more and become more, you are a leader.
—John Quincy Adams

Who is Following You?

Someone once said, Look behind you to see who is following you. If no one is there, then you are probably not a leader. That little saying has always stuck with me as somewhat humorous, but probably accurate. Undoubtedly the most important characteristic of being in leadership is to understand how to be led oneself.

I have been under many leaders in my life. Some of the leaders have been in the arena of education, where I have spent over four decades as an educator. Some leaders have been in the church — pastors, teachers, counselors, and so on. I must say that the leaders who stood out to me the most had similar qualities. They were those who could see the potential in others, and encouraged and challenged them to strive to fulfill their potential. They were also humble individuals who were not afraid to serve those under them. True leaders are not afraid of responsibility, and take ownership of their actions. And most importantly, they know how to follow — whether that is to follow God or follow their superiors.

When Jesus walked the earth, He had a close band of twelve followers. Beyond that, many others (even multitudes) sought to make Him King. All of His followers had varying degrees of commitment, and distinct reasons for wanting His leadership. In fact, even one of His closest disciples betrayed Him. What we don't always think about is the fact that Jesus Himself was a follower. He only did what He saw the Father do, and He only spoke what He heard the Father speak. He followed the leadership of the Holy Spirit. Let's ponder His attitude as leader if we have a line of followers behind us.

One morning, decades ago in the quietness of listening for His voice, I heard Him sing this to me, using the melody from an old familiar song:

Softly, I will lead you softly
Long before you know, then I will show, the way to go.
I will lead you softly, you will be beside Me
We will walk as one, until the day your work is done
And I will lead you there.
Gently, I will lead you gently
For you are My bride, I am your King
I will supply all that you need, everything
I will fill your heart with My love too
You are in Me, I am in you, I am in you.

Whispers of the Divine

Leadership is responsibility. You need to use the ability I have given you in order to respond authentically and lovingly and accurately to people. You represent Me to them as a Christian leader. I guard My sheep jealously, and take very seriously the appointment to leadership and guardianship over My sheep. In order for My sheep to hear My voice from you, you must speak My words from My heart.

Chapter Eighteen

LIFE

There are only two ways to live your life. One is as though nothing is a miracle. The other is as though everything is a miracle.
— Albert Einstein

Live Like Everyone is Watching!

I can still remember a particular day as a young child when I was playing in a schoolyard. It was paved with concrete, and I was stunned when I came upon a tiny plant emerging from a barely visible crack in the cement. What fascinated my young mind was how a fragile green bud could have the strength to burst forth into life amid the lifeless acres of concrete. Somehow the memory of that scene has remained with me all these years, and has encouraged me to embrace the power of life. Even now when my circumstances seem to be stuck between the proverbial rock and a hard place, my mind goes back to that little plant pushing its way into the light, and I am empowered to press on.

My life has certainly had its share of adversity, and I've had many opportunities to want to quit. However, it seems that each time I reached that point, something would come along to remind me of the power that life has. If we have the eyes to see, the miracle of life is everywhere around us.

One year, in the kindergarten class at our school, they incubated some fertilized chicken eggs. In just three weeks, an egg transforms from what is essentially a fertilized yolk into a live, complete chick. It takes a baby chick about 24 hours to break out of its shell. This hatching process is both beautiful and miraculous. I would encourage you to investigate the details of the process because the transformation is a mystery that few know about. It is a living testimony to the power of life.

What about the metamorphosis of the caterpillar into a butterfly? What about the uniqueness of each and every snowflake? Do you know that the dragonfly is the greatest flyer in nature? It can fly forwards, hover, fly backwards, and fly upside down. It can move all four wings in different directions at the same time. Have you ever thought about how a spider spins its web? A spider's silk web is completely elastic, but pound for pound stronger than steel. This silk is one hundred times thinner than human hair.

Have you ever been interested in the month-to-month development of a human being in the womb of a woman? As a woman and mother I found that fascinating, and I once read a book that contained every transaction of human growth and development as it occurs in utero. The innumerable and intricate detail of events from conception to birth is staggering! Truly, the most miraculous part of human life is that we have a biological and temporal life in our physical bodies, but we also have a spiritual and eternal life in the essence of our being — our spirit being. It will indeed take an eternity to unveil all the mysteries of life.

Whispers of the Divine

The world around you is pulsating with My life. Literally every atom is vibrating and resonating to the sound of My voice. I have come that You may have life and have it more abundantly. See Me, know Me, listen to Me. I am all the life you will ever need. When you are feeling dreary and dull, take some time to look outside of yourself to My creation, and praise Me for it. Challenge yourself to seek out something new about Me and what I am doing in the earth. Ask Me what I am doing. Talk to Me the way you would pursue a friend. Allow Me to speak into your days and nights. Be sensitive to the stirrings of My Spirit within you, and act on the things you sense within you.

Picture a river. Picture a river flowing from your innermost being, Picture the immense power of that river because the source is the very throne of the Creator of the Universe. That river flows from His throne to and through your heart! It is the force of life of the Spirit of God. You drink of that river personally which is the same river that I drink of...imagine! We share the same power, the same resource of love, peace, goodness, life and all that the river contains. Allow the river of My Spirit to fill you and flow out of you today. Drink of its deliciousness, and share its goodness with all around you. In prayer you can direct the flow of the power of the river to a particular situation in need of My power and provision. Life is exciting! Life for you is exciting. See the river!

A tree lives from the sap that flows within it. Your physical body lives from the blood that is pumped through it. Your spirit lives from the life force of My eternal Spirit. You truly have no life apart from Me either naturally or spiritually. Once you recognize this, you will understand the necessity of being vitally united to Me. Open yourself up to include Me in all that you think, say and do. This is the quality of eternal life that I desire for you to have in the here and now.

Chapter Nineteen

LIGHT

God is light.
What He speaks is light.
The first thing He created was light.

Asking the Right Questions

When going through darkness, difficulties or troubling times, of course none of you were ever tempted to question: "Why, God, why?" "Why me, God? Why do I deserve this?" "Why is this happening to me? I try so hard to do what's right!" I have to confess that I have asked God a question or two along these lines in my life. Apparently, someone else in history also did.

There is an ancient story in the Bible, which according to scholars, appears in the oldest book of the Bible. It is the Book of Job, and it describes the account of a righteous man who suddenly experienced extraordinary tragedy and loss all at once. It is pretty overwhelming as one of the wealthiest men around to lose thousands of livestock (sheep, camels, oxen, and donkeys) plus all the servants who tended to them, and all of your children in the same day. Then, to make matters worse, Job was physically afflicted from head to toe with severe sores. Job's friends were no help with all their implications of his guilt.

The reality behind the scene was that it had been the adversary, the devil who afflicted Job with all these troubles. God was so assured of Job's devotion to Him, that He allowed this trial to prove Job's unwavering faith. It is no wonder that Job wanted an audience with God to settle the matter. He had a few questions to ask.

The problem with the type of questions that Job asked, and that we may potentially ask, is that within the questions is shrouded some form of accusation against the Creator. Job did in fact eventually have an audience with God. I imagine it was pretty terrifying to hear the booming voice of the Almighty coming out of a whirlwind, challenging Job with questions of His own.

I thought it might be interesting to include some of the questions that God challenged Job with in this section. Bear in mind that God has been so gracious as to reveal wisdom and insights into His creation through subsequent civilizations and generations of humanity, but Job lived long before all those advancements. Even though Job was not able to answer God's questions, the happy ending to the story is that God restored to him double of all that had been taken from him by the enemy.

God asked Job:

- Where were you when I laid the earth's foundations? Tell me if you know.
- Who set its measurements?
- Who stretched a measuring tape on it? On what were its footings sunk; who laid its cornerstone, while the morning stars sang in unison and all the divine beings shouted?
- Who enclosed the sea behind doors when it burst forth from the womb, when I made the clouds its garment, the dense clouds its wrap, when I imposed my limit for it, put on a bar and doors and said, You may come this far, no farther, here your proud waves stop?
- Have you gone to the sea's sources, walked in the chamber of the deep?
- Have death's gates been revealed to you; can you see the gates of deep darkness?
- Have you surveyed earth's expanses? Tell me if you know everything about it?
- Where's the road to the place where light dwells; darkness, where's it located? Can you take it to its territory; do you know the paths to its house?

- Have you gone to snow's storehouses, seen the storehouses of hail that I have reserved for a time of distress, for a day of battle and war?
- What is the way to the place where light is divided up; the east wind scattered over earth?
- Who cut a channel for the downpour and a way for blasts of thunder to bring water to uninhabited land, a desert with no human to saturate dry wasteland and make grass sprout?
- Has the rain a father who brought forth drops of dew? From whose belly does ice come; who gave birth to heaven's frost?
- Can you bind Pleiades' chains or loosen the reins of Orion?
- Can you guide the stars at their proper times, lead the bear with her cubs?
- Do you know heaven's laws, or can you impose its rule on earth?
- Can you issue an order to the clouds so their abundant waters cover you?
- Can you send lightning so that it goes and then says to you, I'm here?
- Who put wisdom in remote places, or who gave understanding to a rooster?
- Who is wise enough to count the clouds, and who can tilt heaven's water containers so that dust becomes mud and clods of dirt adhere?
- Can you hunt prey for the lions, or fill the cravings of lion cubs?
- Who provides food for the raven when its young cry to God?
- Do you know when mountain goats give birth; do you observe the birthing of does?

- Who freed the wild donkey, loosed the ropes of the onager to whom I gave the desert as home, his dwelling place in the salt flats?

- Did you give strength to the horse, clothe his neck with a mane, cause him to leap like a locust, his majestic snorting, a fright?

- Is it due to your understanding that the hawk flies, spreading its wings to the south?

- Or at your command does the eagle soar, the vulture build a nest on high?

As I ponder these questions, I am pretty sure they were all rhetorical, designed to incite awe at the immensity of God's power, or perhaps a reminder of our impotence in light of His omnipotence.

Whispers of the Divine

I am light because I have all knowledge. There is nothing that I do not know. All is exposed before Me as true or fraud. I have all understanding and all wisdom. Therefore, nothing can be hidden from Me. It is good that you let My light shine on you and expose the things in your life that do not resonate with My truth. When you align with My truth about things. Then you are walking in the light. That is why I said in the Epistle of John to walk in the light with others. There are things about yourself that others see which you cannot see. When those are exposed and dealt with properly, then you are cleansed by My blood from all sin. Sin is the darkness causing you to miss the mark of what is true and right.

Chapter Twenty

LOVE

Love is not only something you feel, it is something you do.
—David Wilkerson

He Loves Me. He Loves Me Not.

I imagine that mankind's essential need and search for love began at the beginning of time, as we know it. As humans, for millennia we knew three basic categories of love: erotic love, brotherly love, and familial love. In Greek the corresponding words are: *eros, phileo, and storge. Eros* is physical attraction, or sexual love. *Phileo* is an expressed natural affection, which can be used for friends, family or humanity in general. *Storge* is familial, nurturing love, which expresses concern, support and affection.

When Jesus Christ walked the earth in His ministry, He introduced a new and unique expression of love — the God-kind of love — *agape. Agape* is an undefeatable benevolence and unconquerable goodwill that always seeks the highest good of the other person, no matter what he or she does. It is the self-giving love that gives freely without asking anything in return, and does not consider the worth of its object.

I'd like to share a portion of the words to an old hymn that extols the love of God. *The Love of God* was written by Frederick Martin Lehman (1868-1953). The story told by the author of this song is that the last verse had been found penciled on the wall of a patient's room in an insane asylum after he had been carried to his grave. While it is only supposition that he was the one who adapted the Jewish author's poem to leave us these well-known lines, if the account is true it shows in any case that he highly esteemed the message.

While some of the language is antiquated, written in the year 1917, the essence of the message captures the magnitude of God's love:

THE LOVE OF GOD

The love of God is greater far
Than tongue or pen can ever tell;
It goes beyond the highest star,
And reaches to the lowest hell;
The guilty pair, bowed down with care,
God gave His Son to win;
His erring child He reconciled,
And pardoned from his sin.

Refrain:
Oh, love of God, how rich and pure!
How measureless and strong!
It shall forevermore endure—
The saints' and angels' song.

Could we with ink the ocean fill,
And were the skies of parchment made,
Were every stalk on earth a quill,
And every man a scribe by trade;
To write the love of God above
Would drain the ocean dry;
Nor could the scroll contain the whole,
Though stretched from sky to sky.

We are to be captivated by God's love. We often talk about the love of God, preach and teach about it, sing about it, long to feel it, and hopefully try to demonstrate it in our lives. The thing is, God's love is not an attribute that He has. Love is the essence of His Personhood. He Himself is love. Love is the consummate quality of His self-perpetuating, eternal existence. This is most difficult for the meager capacity of our human brains to grasp. However, we can spiritually experience Him as He dwells in us through His Spirit. I think God Himself best illuminates the topic in the excerpts that follow.

Whispers of the Divine

That I love you, that I love you, that I love you! You have almost NO idea how much I truly love you, but I am teaching you. I am helping you, and I am wooing you. I need you to trust Me. Yes, there is a veil at present, but you can pass through the veil in the Spirit. Even if you can't physically be with Me, we can have sweet fellowship in the Spirit. I love you personally — not for what you do, but for who you are — who I have made you to be. I do take pleasure in being with you also — so much more than you realize at present. But someday you will know in fullness of assurance. You have been waiting for a moment for everything to be different between you and I, but I am gradually changing you. Little by little you are taking back what the enemy has stolen from us. Stay in the Spirit.

My gentle dove, you are beautiful, and I want to comfort you. In all the days, in all the ways My love extends to you as a beautiful sunset touches the vast horizon. It melts into the water and is reflected in its depths. I want to reflect My love in the depths of your heart and fill you with the ocean of My love. The greatness of My love for you cannot be measured, for it is endless. Bask now in the beauty of the sunset. Let it bring you peace and rest.

You think that your heart is not loved. You think that you are not loved because you want someone to touch your heart with love. I want you to look at My human heart on the cross. I allowed My physical heart to be pierced for you. My heart burst because of the spear that was thrust into my side. Your heart feels like it will burst with pain sometimes. Look at the spear piercing my heart for you. Know that whatever touches your heart touches my heart. I lost the divine touch of the Father's heart in that time that I was separated from Him. Divine anguish, divine loss, and divine rejection — I did this for you. I was alienated and separated from the Father so that you could be forever joined to Him and loved by Him. Allow your heart to feel that love now. Accept the divine love and receive it now.

Love. I want to talk to you about love. Love is Who I am. The essence of My being is love. Love is not something I do, or grow in, or express only — it is the essence of My character, my being, my DNA, so to speak. Every thought is love, every word is love, every action is love — only pure love. All of My creativity is love, all of My wisdom is love, all of My expressions are love because it is the composite of all that I am. The light of My being radiates love. Whenever I give, the gift may vary, but it is always a gift from love. The precision of My planning, the strategies, are all love. Even the very atmosphere of heaven radiates love because the energy of My Being, which is love, permeates the atmosphere. When you are here, you will feel love, see love, breathe love, taste love, and be love because you will be transformed into My perfect image and likeness in human form just as your Elder Brother, Jesus. That is My full intention for you — to conform you into the image of Jesus Christ. My desire is a race of love beings — My children, My sons and daughters. When you know Me, you know love. This is what intimacy is, My child, My daughter. You are Mine, you are My love child. Get to know yourself as mine — get to know Me as yours.

I want you to find Me approachable. Your approach to Me is not dependent upon your deeds — good or bad. It depends upon the position that has been secured for you in the Man Christ Jesus. I have accepted all men and women in Him. He alone is perfect in His ways, and He alone made the sacrifice necessary to obtain access to relationship with Me for all eternity.

You have had difficulty being close to even your own parents, your children, your siblings, and even your own spouse. You are introspective in that regard, and constantly examining your acceptability to others. You have expected that My standards are even higher than human standards, and therefore did not anticipate that you could be close to Me. But I am the One Who loves you unconditionally. I loved you before you were born. I prepared the way for you to be in relationship with Me and planned for your adoption when you were far away and estranged from Me. I created you, I know you, and I love you without limit. I want you to focus on My unconditional love for you because you need to be free *from the limitations of love and your feeling of inadequacy when it comes to being loved. I am the One Who will love you completely — frailty and all, failures and all. However, My deepest desire is that you experience that love in freedom and that you become able to reciprocate, for that will be your greatest pleasure in life.*

Chapter Twenty-One

MINISTRY

Ministry is spelled W-O-R-K!
—Kenneth W. Hagin

It is Better to Give

The word ministry actually means service, and those who minister are those who serve others. When we are takers we are the recipients of something. We can all receive love, joy, mercy, peace, or other blessings (material or otherwise.) However, when we are givers we must first *be* or *become* the quality we want to give - such as being loving, joyful, rich, merciful or peaceful, and so forth. That is why it is much better to give than to receive. There is transformation in the giving.

If I receive love but do not give love, I experience it for a while, but then it disappears. If I continually am giving love, then I actually become loving. It is truly given to me more. As I minister mercy, I experience mercy. In order to exude peace to others, I must first have peace within. That is why when we give; it shall be given unto us (Luke 6:38). God is interested in forming His character in us, which is why He encourages us to give. He gives to us in order for us to minister to others.

At the time that God gave His Only Begotten Son, all humanity was doomed to destruction. By giving His only Son, He now has more sons (and daughters) to love Him. The more He gave, the more He received. The more we give, the more we receive. This is the operation of true ministry.

Whispers of the Divine

First and foremost, I want you to love Me as My child. Love Me with all of your heart, soul, mind and strength. I also want you to receive My love for you. Everything else must be a natural outflow of this love relationship. Ministry is a natural outflow of this love relationship, because ministry is loving and serving others, always looking for the best possible outcome. You cannot properly do ministry or service to others without first contacting Me on a deep level. I am the one who sees into the hearts and needs of people, so only I can righteously guide you into the truth of ministry. My people often look for pat answers to problems, or pat solutions to people's issues, but I AM the WAY, so all must look to me first to lead and guide in the way to solve problems and situations. Many people try to do ministry without a genuine relationship with Me in the ministry. I don't mean that they are not saved. I mean that they choose to work independently of My counsel. The most successful people in ministry are the ones who put their relationship with Me first.

Chapter Twenty-Two

PEACE

Peace is liberty in tranquility.
—Marcus Tullius Cicero

Take a chill pill

Shalom is the Hebrew word for peace, and its meaning is profound. *Shalom* indicates completeness, wholeness, health, welfare, safety, soundness, tranquility, prosperity, perfectness, fullness, rest, and harmony. In shalom there is complete absence of any agitation or discord. Strife does not exist, because *shalom* denotes harmonious relationships of all kinds. Just reading this definition allows me to take a deep breath, and feel a sense of rest on the inside.

In the Middle East, *shalom* is the word used in greeting each other or departing from one another. They are saying something like this to each other, I pray that all is well and whole with you. I pray your relationships are harmonious, and that you have an abundance of resources to live on. I pray that nothing is missing or broken in your life.

On my first trip to Israel in 2011, I had the amazing opportunity to spend Shabbat (or Sabbath) in Jerusalem at the Western Wall. The nation of Israel continuously has to deal with some sort of war, terrorism escalation, or political upheaval, and yet their day of rest is an important symbol of Jewish identity. Even in a busy modern world, observant Jews still take time to rest on the Sabbath, just like God did on the seventh day of creation. In their homes they divide and eat challah bread every Friday night; they recite prayers and readings from the Torah, and bless their women and children. They repeat these actions every week, until they become familiar rituals. Though not in a Jewish home, my Shabbat at the Western Wall was exceptional.

There were multitudes gathered at the Western Wall to pray that evening. As the daylight diminished and dusk settled on the city, there was both stillness in the air and yet a holy joy erupting at the Wall. The doves settled into the crevices in the huge stones, and a powerful Presence of God descended on the evening. I remember thinking, It is good; it is well with my soul. I will never forget that moment. It was a profound experience of palpable peace!

How does one find this place of peace, especially in our world so filled with anxiety, pressure, and discord? *Shalom* is a gift — it was given to us to receive. Jesus Christ speaking to His disciples before His departure to heaven said in John 14:27,

"I am leaving you with a gift — peace of mind and heart. And the peace I give is a gift the world cannot give. So don't be troubled or afraid." Peace is a gift to you. Receive it today. Let peace pervade your circumstances, your relationships, or your inner conflicts. Let peace settle down on the inside and bring wholeness in your life.

> Now may the God of peace Himself sanctify you completely; and may your whole spirit, soul, and body be preserved blameless at the coming of our Lord Jesus Christ.
> —1 Thessalonians 5:23

Whispers of the Divine

My disciples were concerned about being left or abandoned by Me in a difficult situation. You have also had that concern deeply embedded in your heart. I would like you to put that to rest once and for all, and live in the gift of PEACE that I have for you. The world cannot give you the kind of peace that I can because everything in this life is temporary, and will someday pass away. But what I have to offer you will never pass away. Every gift that I have to give you will only make you stronger, more well, more equipped, more wise, more joyful. I never remove that which is good for you, I only add to it. You can honestly rest in Me in every situation and circumstance because I am MORE than enough, and MORE than able, and MORE than willing to aid and assist you. That is why you can have peace. So now let go of all doubt, fear, anxiety, insecurity, and allow My peace to flood your heart. You will know completeness as never before.

Peace, My child. Learn peace from Me. Trust Me. I will fulfill the desires of your heart when you can look to Me alone. When I am your desire above all else, and you cease striving, then you can know peace. To know peace is to have fulfillment, regardless of the circumstances. What you desire is good, but even what you desire is flawed on the earth. There can be no completeness and fullness without Me in the midst. Yes, continue holding precious your desires, but hold them up to Me and allow Me to fulfill them in the right time and place. Rest, rest in Me. Think about Me in your daily life. Allow Me to fill the moments of your life and then you will have contentment. If you could only see Me for who I truly am. I AM the fulfillment of every desire you could ever have. Seeing Me takes practice, but you can do it.

Peace is not meekness or weakness. Peace is strength. Peace is the ability to enforce order into life — the power to make things go the way that they should go. Peace makes wrong things right.

Chapter Twenty-Three

PERFECTION

Perfection consists not in doing extraordinary things, but in doing ordinary things extraordinarily well.
—Angelique Arnauld

Nobody's Perfect

It has taken me almost an entire lifetime of wrestling with the idea of perfection to finally come to the place where I can accept that I am perfectly imperfect. Both of my parents were perfectionists, so I was trained to also want things to be in accordance with the highest standards of propriety. The house we lived in was impeccably organized and clean. The yard was flawlessly manicured. I was encouraged to be a model student in school, and my grades were always in the A range.

Especially being raised in Southern California, our society continually broadcasted the need to look flawless, have the ideal partner, raise model children, and pursue an admirable profession. Such pressure to live up to! There really isn't anything intrinsically wrong with any of those things; however, the problem arises when we begin to think less of ourselves if and when we don't achieve the ideal standards we have set up. So, when I actually came to the point of wanting to accept God into my life, I transferred all of my expectations of perfection onto Him. After all, He most certainly is perfect, and would want me to be perfect also. What I didn't understand was that God's definition of being perfect was entirely different from mine. He defines perfect as "mature and complete."

I am perfect because I was designed and created by the One who does all things perfectly. I am uniquely and perfectly who I am supposed to be — not to be confused with who I think (or who others think) I should be. I am made in His image. The only way to discover who I am is to learn who He is. I am known by Him, so in order to know myself, I need to know Him.

Am I flawed? Most certainly! However now, instead of rejecting my value when I face my imperfections, I can lean into His perfect grace and love for me, which enables me to overcome the need to perfect myself. He gives us space to breathe, to grow, to mature, and to become aligned with His perfect design for our lives. Remember:

> If one man's sin brought a reign of death—that's Adam's legacy—how much more will those who receive grace in abundance and the free gift of redeeming justice reign in life by means of one other man—Jesus the Anointed.
>
> Romans 5:17 (VOICE)

Whispers of the Divine

You have such a problem with wanting to be perfect and right and not fail. All of humanity failed through Adam in the Garden of Eden. Read Romans 5:17 again, and meditate on this truth. You can never be perfect, righteous, or good without Me. The sooner you abandon your need to feel perfect for perfection's sake, the sooner you will understand. I have asked you to be perfect in the sense that you would mature in your love relationship with Me. I have not asked you to be perfect in the sense that you never make mistakes, or fail in your attempt at holiness. Holiness comes from wholeness, which comes from integrity. Integrity is your completeness in Me. I have provided that for you. Enter into that which I have given you simply by your fellowship with me. Your fellowship and communion with Me is not something you do, it is something you allow to happen by submitting to My Spirit. You can do that — you know how to do that. It is not complicated, but it will require you to change your mindset about this. Become like a child. Just be My child.

Any time that you allow a situation or circumstance or person to appear greater in your heart than My strength or ability to deal with it, that is an idol. Be careful as you come to Me in prayer to first acknowledge who I am — as they did in the book of Acts 4. When you magnify Me first, then idolatry is difficult. When you see how big and capable I am, your focus will not be on the problem or the issue or the pressure you feel. Seeking perfection can be an idol. Perfection can be your idol. When your prayer becomes a means to attain perfection for your life, that is idolatrous. Your goal should be to know Me — nothing less, nothing more. You will never live problem-free in this life. I have told you that in the world you will have tribulation. Don't seek a life without difficulty. That is the wrong motivation for prayer. Seek a life of victory over the difficulty. I said that you can be of good cheer because I have overcome for you. I never promised a life of comfort and ease, but I have sent the promised Comforter to be with you in times of trial.

Perfectionism — this plagues many of My people. Regardless of how much one does for Me, or tries not to sin, or other such actions to lead a spiritual life, there can never be perfection. I don't look for perfection - I look for obedience. What did I say in My word? Show mercy, do kindness and walk humbly with your God. If it were possible to be perfect in all your ways, then I would have never sent My Son because you could achieve perfection on your own. The Law proved that humanity was unable to save itself. I sent One to save you. You think that now that you are saved that you will achieve perfection. Never on this side of the veil as long as you live in the frail human body. That is what redemption is all about. I have redeemed your spirit, I am sanctifying your soul, and one day your body will be fully redeemed to immortality. But not yet. Accept your frailty in human form as Paul did and said that he gloried in his weakness because then My grace was sufficient for his strength.

Be your best self today. Be who I have created you to be. Be in the splendor of the moment because I breathe into you, I stand with you, I draw you into My purposes for life. You are perfection when you abide in Me. Settle into that. Settle into your home in Me today. There is rest in that. Perfection is simply being who you are in Me and doing the will of the Father — nothing more, nothing less.

Chapter Twenty-Four

PERSPECTIVE

We can complain because rose bushes have thorns,
or rejoice because thorn bushes have roses.
– Abraham Lincoln

Positioned for the Right Perspective

When you think of the word holy what does it mean to you? What emotion does it evoke deep inside? Do you see halos over the heads of would be saints? I would venture to say that many different definitions and connotations could emerge from this inquiry. However, the only perspective that truly matters is that which God has. It is He who said that we should be holy because He is holy.

Biblically speaking, holy means set apart for an intended purpose. In the Old Testament, the kings and priests were set apart or sanctified for a particular service to the people on behalf of God. The articles for worship in the Tabernacle were set apart for very specific ceremonial purpose. In common usage, something holy could be an article of clothing like a wedding gown which is sanctified because it is set apart for a specific purpose — the wedding ceremony.

The first mention in the Bible of this sanctification, consecration, dedication, and purification is in Exodus 29:21, and it mentions the blood and the oil which were used in the process. Whoever or whatever is sanctified enters into a new state, belonging to God and to be used wholly and solely by Him in the way He sees fit.

The Blood of Jesus makes us holy by position. The oil or anointing of the Holy Spirit makes us holy by possession. Jesus' blood positions us in the Presence of the Father, in forgiveness, in redemption, in healing, in deliverance, and in wholeness. He positions us in the Anointed Holy Christ. The Holy Spirit possesses us and imparts God's holiness to us!

The purpose for this wonderful setting apart is to keep us safe, right, good, and free from all that would harm us. What the Holy Father has birthed in us is His holy love, holy joy, holy peace, holy longsuffering, holy kindness, holy goodness, holy faithfulness, holy gentleness, and holy self-control. His perspective on holiness is wholeness in every way.

Whispers of the Divine

What I want to tell you about demonic versus the Holy Spirit has to do with your perspective. You are seated with Me in heavenly places — high above the activity of the enemy. You must see yourself there and allow the perspective of your position in Christ (Me) to influence your thinking. Many of My people make much ado about the activity of the enemy. That is what he wants — the focus to be on him. Lift your sights and thoughts as it says in the book of Colossians to heavenly places where you are seated with Me. There you will hear the voice of the Holy Spirit more clearly because there will be no interference of the enemy's voice. Let's practice that now. Visualize heaven and the realities of heaven.

Chapter Twenty-Five

REST

Rest and be thankful.
—William Wadsworth

Mayday! Mayday!

I remember the perfect picture of rest during a plane ride from Denver to Los Angeles. There was a lot of turbulence — the kind of turbulence that jostles and rattles everything in the overhead bins. It seemed like the plane was a leaf being blown in the wind — swaying from side to side and dropping up and down. I admit I was slightly shaken, and I was probably clutching the armrests a little too tightly. Then, I glanced over the isle to a woman across from me. She had a swaddled baby cradled in her arms and nestled in her breast. She was gently rocking the child and whispering, Sh-sh-sh. The child was sleeping in her arms and completely unaware of the perilous flight. It was then that I felt the Lord direct my attention to the fact that this is how He wants me to rest in Him even in the midst of turbulent circumstances. What is that saying, "A picture is worth a thousand words"?

I began dance lessons at three years old. I'm not sure why, except now I know that at the very core of my identity, I am a dancer. Maybe I used to dance around the house when I was just a tiny little girl — I don't really know for certain. What I do know is that my maternal grandmother started me in dance lessons of all kinds — tap, ballet, jazz, and so on. There were recitals and performances. I have memories of being on stage in costumes of all types. In elementary school I was part of an Irish dance group that competed in Los Angeles each year.

This passion for dance continued throughout my life and filled my days with the joy of movement. More lessons, more classes in Afro-Cuban, modern dance (now called Contemporary style) and folk dancing from every country. Dance eventually became my minor in college. After much reflection, I decided to become an educator instead of a professional dancer, but even then I joined dance groups and performed in various seasons of my life. At one point, I actually started writing a book using the principles of dance as a guide for life. Maybe I'll finish writing it one day!

Dance has taught me a lot of lessons in life. My Creator knows this. He made me to be a very kinesthetic person. Even so, it was a little surprising to me, and brilliant of Him, to use a dance analogy while speaking to me of rest.

Whispers of the Divine

Come away with Me for awhile. Sit with me. Be still. Let your heart rest in My Presence. You are troubled with so many things. You need to center in Me — be centered with your attention on Me. It is like doing turns in dance — if you don't find a focal point, you will get dizzy, off-kilter, and possibly fall. I must be your focal point. Make this a priority.

You have not practiced My Presence. You have been busy doing other things like praying, reading the Bible, and so forth without first waiting on Me. Rest, rest, rest is essential in coming into My presence. Rest from your own efforts. Let me take the initiative. Relax in Me, and let Me lead the way. You so much want to do it right that you have often forfeited the actual experience of My presence. Let go, let go, let it be, let Me be in you. Let Me be what I want to be to you, don't try to be something for Me. I have made you who you are, I accept you for who you are. Let Me be in you. Trust, rest, relax, breathe, quiet yourself, be easy, like a child. Practice this. Don't be afraid to let go — don't be afraid to let go. You can trust me. I can take care of you. You are used to working so hard to take care of yourself, you are not accustomed to letting someone care for you. I want to do this for you, but you must allow Me. I want you to enjoy your life more. It is not always a battle, a fight, a work. It can be a joy. You are too worried about the future. Let go of that worry.

You need to rest from the many fretting and struggling behaviors you are in. Let it all go! Learn to rest in My presence. Truly, truly rest. Meaning, the only effort that you should be making is to enter into My will. Rest in my plan. If you struggle, struggle to press into Me and My strength, My plan, My purpose. When you are in that position, then I am able to do what I want to do for you. Press into the rest in Me.

I want to take you into a deeper rest, a more profound state of rest. I want to enhance the acuity of your spiritual senses to vibrancy and energy for execution in power. I want to reveal to you the complete state of unity that we have in the spirit. I want to move you along the path to becoming stronger and stronger each day. The more you yield to Me, the deeper your rest will be. You have no idea the depths of creativity that are available to you — the gladness, the joy, the complete satisfaction in Me. So many are striving to find all of this externally, but the journey is an internal one — deep into the recesses of My Spirit where the operation of My Kingdom excels. Do you want more power for ministry? Go deeper in Me. Do you want more peace and satisfaction? Go deeper in Me. There is a Kingdom that awaits you, My dear. Ha-ha-ha! Do you realize how many movies you have seen in your lifetime with this theme of the princess and the prince living happily ever after? Happily ever after is inside you. Ha-ha-ha!

Come to Me. Just be with Me. So much of your life has been spent in striving to be good, to be perfect, to be faithful and true. I only ask you to come to Me and lean on Me; learn of Me. You can do nothing apart from Me. All striving is futile. Trust Me, trust Me, trust Me. You will find complete fulfillment and rest in your abiding in Me. You don't have to be strong. In your weakness, I am made strong. Rest in me. You are learning how to yield and surrender. There is no greater joy than this.

How many colors are in your world? How many shades of blue, purple, red? How many animals and insects and birds and fish are there? How deep is the ocean? How high is the sky? How big is life? You feel so small and frail and yes even hopeless and helpless at times. How vast is My life and My love for you? It is fathomless and endless and priceless and yet very present to you. Come to Me with your pain, with your failures, with your emptiness and I will fill you. Would you not come to a table to eat if you were hungry? Would you not come to a bed for rest if you were tired? Come to Me — I will feed you and fill you and give you rest for your weary soul.

The work of the Holy Spirit has been to place you in Me. You were present in Me when I died on the cross and when I was raised from the dead. Your position before the Father is in Me. But to remain in Me, you must continually partake of My Word, and My eternal covenant of sacrifice for you. When you drink of My Spirit, you are partaking of Me because We are one. Activate the Spirit within you, and you will activate your presence in Me. When you engage the language of the Holy Spirit, you are deep inside of Me, because He plumbs the depths of Me. Any time that you flow in the unction of the Holy Spirit, you are moving inside of Me. We are one. My blood gives you access to Me. My Spirit gives you access to Me. Even breathing out My name gives you access to Me. However, to abide — to remain in Me means that you forsake all things that would distract you from My presence. First you must learn to rest in Me, and then you can learn to abide in Me. Cease from your labors, and come to rest in Me.

Chapter Twenty-Six

REWARD

But without faith it is impossible to please Him, for he who comes to God must believe that He is, and that He is a rewarder of those who diligently seek Him.
— Hebrews 11:6

Gratification or Reward?

I used to read this verse in Hebrews and focus on the part about faith being needed to please God. One day, however, I noticed the second part of the verse, and I was surprised to see that I also needed to believe that God is a rewarder. It pleases our Father for us to believe that He wants to reward us for seeking Him.

I have two children — the elder by four years is female, and the younger, male. My son was adopted right after he was born, and I knew very little about his genetics or birth parents at the time. I was just thrilled to bring home this sweet new baby boy.

It didn't take long to awaken to the reality that there were some issues. Very early on in elementary school he was tested and it was discovered that he not only had ADHD, but also auditory and visual learning deficiencies.

I am an educator myself, so I definitely felt that with understanding and effort we could overcome these challenges. It was a long and difficult journey; even applying all of the information and skills I had learned by gaining certification as an educational therapist.

One of the compensations I had put in place to redirect negative behaviors was to provide a reward at the end of a school day if he was able to choose the appropriate responses all day. It was my earnest desire to be able to reward him. I probably wanted to give him the reward more than he wanted to receive it. I can remember several days when I picked him up from school only to discover that right at the end of the day he made a wrong choice. My disappointment was so keen, that it was heartbreaking to not be able to reward him.

When I think of my own longing to reward my son, it helps me understand to just a tiny extent the enormous desire on the part of our Heavenly Father to reward us as we diligently seek Him. My intimate knowledge of God does not come via casual effort, but rather by diligence — day by day.

Tomorrow my son will turn thirty-four years old, and I could not be more proud of the man he has become. When he turned eighteen, he joined the U.S. Army for four years — most of which he spent in Fairbanks, Alaska. He is now married, a father and a homeowner (dog included.) He put himself through college, and most recently completed a two-year course to become a licensed nurse. He has shown me that in spite of his learning challenges, his consistent effort has brought him great rewards.

Whispers of the Divine

One of the more difficult things for you and others to do is to defer self-gratification. Especially in your culture, there is much pressure to accept instant reward for one's desires. There is a broad acceptance of the fact that self is deserving of rewards. I do most certainly believe in reward, as my kingdom is built upon this principle, and I am a rewarder of those who diligently seek Me. The key word is diligently. There is consistent effort before reward. The other element to this equation is faith. You must believe that I am and that I will reward diligence. It takes faith to defer the pursuit of instant gratification in exchange for everlasting reward.

Chapter Twenty-Seven

RIGHTEOUSNESS

*Our works do not generate righteousness, rather our
righteousness in Christ generates works.*
—Martin Luther

The Law That Supersedes

Does God's word get a grand reception in my life? Does it have such prominence in me that it produces phenomenal amounts of spiritual wealth that continually flows out to enrich those around me? As soon as the inner desire for righteousness is present within me, the Holy Spirit will immediately fill it with His own energy and bring the soul to victory.

The book of Romans in the Bible is one that I have studied repeatedly over decades. It is so rich and deep in revelation that the possibilities for encouragement in our Christian walk are endless. In particular, many years ago I needed to understand how the "law of life" (which is mentioned in Romans 8:2) functioned in my everyday experience. So, I simply asked God that question. The following illustration is what helped me to understand.

We all know that what holds us on this twirling ball of dirt called earth is the law of gravity. Without the law of gravity we would, at the very least, have difficulty being earthbound. And yet, in modern times we have seen remarkable suspension of this law in planes, jets, satellites, rockets and a space station. The simple explanation as to how this is possible is that the law of thrust and lift supersede the law of gravity, enabling heavy metal objects to take flight. Likewise, the law of the Spirit of life has superseded the law of sin and death in our inherited, lower Adamic nature. We now have an entirely new nature from Christ.

The law of God is His will to make all things right and good. God is the source of all life. His life is like the power of electricity flowing. If there is resistance, it breaks the flow and life cannot be conducted. What breaks the flow in us is the law of sin and death. Sin and death is the result of a will being raised up in opposition to the flow of God's life. In Lucifer's rebellion against God, sin (iniquity) was conceived for the first time. Never before had any will challenged the perfect and good law of life flowing from the Almighty.

Fast forward to the Garden of Eden. When Adam and Eve yielded to the Serpent's (fallen Lucifer's) will for them — to challenge God's instruction about eating the fruit of the tree of the knowledge of good and evil — the law of sin and death entered them. From them, the law of sin and death was passed on to all of mankind.

However, at the appointed time the Anointed Savior came and lived His life in perfect submission to the will of the Father. The Man Christ Jesus legally had the law of life operating on His behalf. By taking the punishment for Adam's sin, He transacted an exchange of death for life. God's justice will not allow Him to accept a second payment for sin. Now the agents of sin and death no longer bind anyone who is born of the Spirit and life! We no longer have to be earthbound but are free to soar into the heavenly realm! Jesus Christ has made all things right again!

Whispers of the Divine

You are damaged, distressed and unaware of the dignity that I have given you. Like a prisoner who has been repeatedly beaten down, your life of sin has beaten you down. That is why I offer righteousness. When you do what is right it gives you might. It gives you power within yourself to be elevated in thought and in deed. Accept My righteousness. There is a reservoir of Kingdom righteousness within those who have received Me as their King. Hail Me as King in every part of your life. Don't accept failure — I cannot fail. I am with you forever, even until the end of the ages.

Chapter Twenty-Eight

SPIRIT LIFE

What is our spiritual life? A love union with Jesus, in which the divine and the human give themselves completely to one another.
— Mother Teresa

The Fifth Dimension

I don't know if you are a fan of science fiction, but it's not my favorite genre. However, I can appreciate that the creators of sci-fi books and movies go to great lengths to draw our imaginations into other dimensions. The amazing thing about being human, created in the image of God, is that we too may live life in another dimension. Most of us meander through life in the four dimensions of space and time in this natural world. This was not the original plan. When God formed man out of the dust of the ground, He then breathed His Spirit life into him, and man became capable of supernatural life. It was only later through rejecting God's plan that mankind was subject to spiritual separation from God, which also had the consequence of physical death.

Imagine the perspective that God has on life. The Bible tells us that He sees the end from the beginning.[1] He lives in a Kingdom outside of the confines of time and space. In the Gospel of John, it tells of a man named Nicodemus who questioned Jesus about how he could experience the Kingdom of God. Jesus answered him by saying that he would have to be born of the Spirit.[2] Basically Jesus was telling Nicodemus that His Kingdom was in another dimension — a spiritual, not a physical, dimension. Jesus repeatedly stated that His Kingdom was not of this world.

The Bible has many verses that talk about the spirit realm. There are stories of prophets in the Old Testament like Elijah and Elisha, who saw remarkable things in the Spirit realm, like angel armies and chariots of fire. There are numerous accounts of angelic visitations in both the Old and New Testament. In the New Testament, the last book written by the apostle John is filled with visions of this other dimension. The book of Ephesians specifically states that we are seated with Christ in heavenly places.[3] So the Kingdom of God is not observable with physical senses, because it is a spiritual kingdom and experienced within our spirits. As Christians, we live in two worlds — the natural and the supernatural.

How can we become sensitive to and aware of this spiritual dimension? First, we must be born of the Spirit of God. We can only gain access by having our spirit beings regenerated by the Holy Spirit. Also, being baptized in the Holy Spirit awakens our spiritual senses to the spirit realm and infuses awareness in us to the supernatural realm that permeates this natural realm.

To what purpose is vision into the spiritual realm? It enables and empowers us to be witnesses to what Jesus is doing now and to partner with Him through the Holy Spirit to continue the work that He began when He walked on the earth. Just as Jesus saw what the Father was doing and acted on that, through the spirit we can observe what Jesus is doing and be His hands, feet and voice in this natural realm.

As I was contemplating the partnership we have in the natural and supernatural, I was prompted to write this prose:

> P u l s a t i n g light with outstretched
> human life invading the universe —
> See how heaven tumbles toward earth
> In an ever-increasing tender caress
> From the h e a r t of god.
>
> B r e a t h e... expanding the consciousness of time —
> Inhale... Exhale...
>
> Light years are moments away in the realm of the
> spirit. Here and there — we find ourselves together
> In both worlds.
> Dust and Glory

Whispers of the Divine

The Father has generated all life from Himself. He is the pure Existent One, the Eternal One. I am the Living Word, the expression of His being, and through the power of the Resurrection, you too have been given eternal life. It can never be rescinded, but you can refuse it. Your weakness is not a consideration, only My power and the power of the Resurrection. We are forever joined in spirit. You forever belong to Me. That is why you can never be alone. Our lives are forever merged for all eternity. Your existence on earth is brief at best, and the decisions you make while in your mortal body do affect your eternity. So be cognizant of this, and rejoice in your security.

Let's talk about your body: Who gives you breath, who designed your autoimmune system to function, who arranged for every chemical and electromagnetic action to spontaneously ignite? Who does? I- your Creator. Who has planned each day of your life and records your words, your thoughts, and your actions in a book? Who counts the hairs on your head, and who captures your tears in a bottle? I do — the Bishop of your soul. Who prepares a place for you in heaven? Who sits at the right hand of the Father interceding for you? I AM all in all. I AM all in your life. And yes, I will answer your prayer to enable you to see this, even in the hard times. I long for the day when you allow yourself to leave the natural and allow yourself to flow in the spiritual and supernatural all of the time. You are still dominated by natural things. You will be living in this world and will have a natural life as long as you are in your body, but you can live in the dimension of the spirit all the time, even while in this body. .

Allow My Spirit to flow within you like a river. You don't control a river unless you want to dam it up. But if you allow it to flow freely then it will take its own course to the open sea. If I am the open sea and the depths of My love are as deep as the great Pacific Ocean, you will want to join Me there. Just take today, and gently let your awareness be on My Spirit within. Let Me take you where

I will today, and don't try so hard. You will be surprised at the release. Don't plan out your day for once, just let it be in My life today.

The more you depend upon Me and the less you depend upon yourself, the more satisfying and invigorating your life will be. You think this is not possible, but it is entirely possible because I am eternal and My Spirit is eternal. There is no pause — no separation to the constant flow of life in the spirit realm. As easily as you connect to your own thoughts, you can just as easily connect to the flow in the Spirit. You think that you have to analyze and judge the validity of the flow in the Spirit, and that is what keeps you from receiving. Be as a child. Be accepting of My flow for you. You can trust Me.

Be consistent. Be consistently aware of these truths. You have known them for many years, but still you cling to the natural rather than the supernatural. You were designed to live the physical life in the flesh, but the rest of your life — your mind, your emotions, your will — should be dictated by the supernatural life of your spirit. Even your physical body can respond to the supernatural life in your spirit when activated by the power of the Holy Spirit. You must learn to govern yourself by the truths that you know and not just know the truths themselves. As with all things, it profits nothing to know something and not to apply it. Do this, and you will do well, My child.

What I am doing is what I have always done. I am loving you into wholeness. My child, I love you with all of My being. I gave My entire life for you. What you are to do is to receive that. I know you will ask Me what is blocking you, and I will show you by revelation. Stay tuned to Me in your heart, in your spirit where we are one. Don't allow the ruminations of your mind to take over. I have given you a spirit of power, love and a disciplined mind. Keep bringing your mind to Me during the day when you find it wandering to other things. Center on the spirit in you, for that is where I dwell. I reside within. Could we be any closer? Yes, we drink of the same Spirit. He is the Spirit of My Father and your Father. He is the life-giving One. All life flows from His mighty throne. You are His child. He conceived you by His Spirit. You will always be His because no one can take you out of His hand. Neither death, nor life, nor things created, nor height, nor depth, nor any created thing — including that which is evil — can ever remove you from His heart. Now, be at peace.

Chapter Twenty-Nine

STILLNESS

Be still, and know that I am God.
—Psalm 46:10

My Tree House

I connect with God the Creator in His creation. I love the water, the mountains, and the fields. However, I especially connect with trees. I don't know why, I just do. In the area where I live there are multitudes of trees. We have numerous tall pine trees with pinecones that keep the squirrels busy. There are magnificent magnolia trees strewn with gloriously large white blossoms. Jacaranda trees spread their velvety purple carpet on the ground. Eucalyptus trees with rugged, resin-dripping bark grow along the walkways of our complex. There are even a variety of lone fruit trees scattered here and there — fig, loquat, cherry, apple, and peach, to name a few. Above all, we have thousands of majestic oak trees. Our town is named after them.

Every day I walk my dog several times, and it is a joy to stroll among the ample varieties of shrubs, bushes, and hedges laden with flowers. I may get a whiff of honeysuckle here, and breathe in the fragrance of a rose there. Nevertheless, my very favorite place is a spot that is the home of an enormous oak tree. The massive rough trunk emerges from the ground in grandeur, supporting voluptuous green-leafed branches that stretch out in all directions for yards and yards. I wonder sometimes how they can reach so far with no apparent support — only the air underneath.

As I stand beneath this tree, I find myself breathless with awe. I dare not move. Not wanting to speak, I stand in stillness. In this stillness, I sense life exuding from every cell of the oak. Although it is motionless, it seems to oscillate with waves of comfort and majesty. I can almost hear it whisper, I've got you covered. I feel safe. It's like being home. I feel at peace. It is as if

God the Creator is speaking to me. I am not thinking, analyzing, or planning. I am only aware. In the stillness I hear His voice and I am able to trust.

Whispers of the Divine

Stillness is an attitude of the heart more than anything else. It is a sense of trust, humility, and abandon to the care of another. It is like being home. You feel welcomed, at ease, comfortable, relaxed. I want all my children to feel this way when they are with Me. Focus on Me, not the state of stillness. I want to be your place of familiarity.

Stillness is not striving; it is waiting upon Me. It is allowing all of your attention and energy to be in My presence. It is quietness of the soul and allowing the flow of the Holy Spirit to gently envelope you. It is leaving everything behind and moving into My presence. It is breathing with My Spirit and knowing Who I am. All is well in My Presence because I am the great I AM. Nothing is outside of my ability or wisdom or life or truth. I am GOOD. You can partake of My goodness when you are still. Do this, and it will be well with you. You will find the answers you seek in the stillness.

Chapter Thirty

SUPERNATURAL

The natural plus the supernatural make an explosive force for God.
— Kenneth W. Hagin

The Queen's Anointing

Not too long ago, I watched the Netflix series entitled *The Crown* about England's royalty. In particular, I was impressed with the scene of the ceremony in which the Queen receives her anointing. It was stunning, and caused me to think of the solemnity regarding the responsibility one has in the use of power from God. From that point on in her life, she was not only her personal self as Elizabeth, but she was empowered to rule as a royal over a kingdom.

Most scriptures in the Old Testament regarding an anointing refer to a pouring over and rubbing in with oil, in order to consecrate or set apart a king or priest into office. It is an external and outward application. This anointing empowered them to do the supernatural work of the Almighty. However, the anointing in the scripture Isaiah 10:27 refers to a deliverance from the threats and burden of the Assyrians who were against God's people. This anointing is used to destroy the yoke of bondage, and is an inward fullness coming from a richness of the Holy Spirit, which causes the very yoke of bondage to burst.

The analogy of a yoke refers to that of oxen. Such a yoke would be unable to go around the neck because of the fatness and fullness, of the lusty richness of the oil — making one full of youthful vigor, strong and robust. The anointing comes from a personal, deeply private encounter with the Holy Spirit in the fellowship and communion that one establishes in spending time with Him. When the anointing of the Holy Spirit comes upon someone, He enables that person to engage in power beyond natural ability:

> You have an anointing. You received it from
> Him, and His anointing remains on you. You do
> not need any other teacher. But as His anointing
> instructs you in all the essentials (all the truth
> uncontaminated by darkness and lies), it teaches
> you this: Remain connected to Him.
> 1 John 2:27 (VOICE)

Whispers of the Divine

I am present in all the manifestations of my Presence and Power — so yes, in the water from the rock, in the cloud and in the fire as well as other manifestations. I will be present with you as you release My Presence through prayer, faith, your confessions, declaration of the Word, laying on of hands and the anointing. I desire to express Myself through my children to the world, just as I was an expression of the Father to the world. Please allow Me to live My LIFE through you. You need to be intentional about this, or you will default to the natural. As you build momentum in the Spirit and giving place to the supernatural, it will become more natural to you and then the natural will seem unnatural. The supernatural is actually easier for you — although now it seems to require more effort — because you were designed to operate in the supernatural flow of life, and not only the natural.

Chapter Thirty-One

THE BLOOD

The blood was shed to unite us to God.
—Andrew Murray

A Drop of Blood

There are some people who faint at the mere sight of a drop of blood. Others cannot get enough of blood and gore. One thing is for certain: blood elicits a strong reaction in us. The Bible certainly doesn't shrink from this topic, and in fact it is the blood, which is the very life and power of the Good News. The blood of Christ purchased remission from sin, freedom from guilt and punishment, and restoration of our relationship with Father God.

In the Garden of Eden, Adam and Eve were the offspring of the Living God. They walked and talked with Him in the cool of the day, until that fateful day when they rebelled against God and forfeited their relationship with Him. The result was spiritual separation and eventually physical death.

The man Christ Jesus was 'fathered' from the Spirit of the Living God. The book of Romans in chapter 5 tells us:

> [12]When Adam sinned, sin entered the entire human race. His sin spread death throughout all the world, so everything began to grow old and die, for all sinned. [15] And what a difference between man's sin and God's forgiveness! For this one man, Adam, brought death to many through his sin. But this one man, Jesus Christ, brought forgiveness to many through God's mercy. [17] The sin of this one man, Adam, caused death to be king over all, but all who will take God's gift of forgiveness and acquittal are kings of life because of this one man, Jesus Christ. [18]

Yes, Adam's sin brought punishment to
all, but Christ's righteousness makes men
right with God, so that they can live.
                    Romans 5:12, 15, 17-18 (TLB)

The Bible informs us in the book of Leviticus that life is in the blood. It is amazing to learn simple biological facts about how blood functions in our bodies. The flow of blood touches every other cell in our bodies, supplying nourishment and carrying off waste products. Think about the fact that when the Holy Spirit raised Jesus from the dead, He not only restored every cell in Christ's body to a mortal state, but to a state of immortality. Just as our physical blood brings life to our bodies, the blood of Jesus releases spiritual life into our spirits. We cannot be spiritually alive without the cleansing power of the blood of Jesus.

The blood of the resurrected Christ, which was poured out on the mercy seat is a most powerful entity. His blood is alive It eternally speaks on our behalf. The blood has cleansed and will continue to cleanse the sin and darkness of every human being from now into eternity. This unprecedented covenant is held between God the Father and the Man Christ Jesus on behalf of all mankind. It can never fail. When this cleansing is received by faith, it has the power to regenerate one's spirit into eternal life. We can remind ourselves of this during the taking of communion.

Communion is a prophetic drama that releases the power of the covenant!

The blood of divinity and of humanity co-mingled in the God-man Jesus Christ of Nazareth. The DNA — fully human and fully divine, converged in the body of Him Who was from the beginning, and Who was made flesh. This Holy One drank fully of the cup of the wrath of God against the nature and the power of sin, which had been enabled to destroy His creation. He drank every last drop. He drank it to the end, letting wrath war against sin until sin succumbed to the power of God and was consumed in Him. Now He offers a cup that brims with life, grace and redemption. Luke 22:20 says, "This cup's for you." When you drink this cup, you can be free from the power of sin to destroy you!

Whispers of the Divine

Just one drop of My blood is so pure and so powerful that it is able to cleanse you of all sin. Just one drop of My blood — just one drop — just one drop. You have seen the list of your sins as insurmountable, but I am telling you that just one drop of MY blood is so concentrated with goodness, with grace, with purity and power that it cleanses and purifies and glorifies and sanctifies you from all defilement. Come to Me and confess your faults, your sins, your transgressions, your iniquities, and I will cleanse them all. You can be so free! Ha- ha- ha! It is for this that I came! I came to seek and save that which was lost — your innocence was lost. I came to destroy the works of the devil. You were enslaved — now you can be free! I can obliterate the works of the devil in your life by ONE DROP OF MY BLOOD! My blood on the mercy seat has been glorified for all eternity. The power of My blood shall never diminish or cease to exist. I am eternally glorified.

You are stuck in the realm of the accusatory. You fail to feel accepted because you feel accused. It cannot be both ways. You either feel accepted or accused. You are forever measuring yourself on the inside to what you perceive on the outside in other's lives. This is a strategy of the enemy to keep you isolated and feeling unacceptable. It is also a snare because then you feel like you must do something to earn your acceptability or to be embraced by others or to please others. This is the snare of the enemy for you because it leads to man-pleasing, which is sin. You only have to please Me, and I am already pleased with you. I have already accepted you, and you are not accused. You may stand before the throne of the Father with confidence in your justification by My blood. Believe in the blood. Believe in the blood. Believe in the blood — it speaks on your behalf. I Myself am pleading your innocence before the Father as I make intercession for you. Do not allow the enemy to accuse you of your guilt any longer. You are free from guilt. Even when you do those things that you feel or know are not right, you can run to Me and be made right by the blood. The blood speaks for you. I am your mediator. I mediate your innocence. Do you understand? You are innocent, and not guilty regardless. Regardless of what you do or do not do that may lead you out of My will, you can always come back. The simple act of returning to Me is your repentance. It is the act of turning away from what you know to not be right and making the deliberate act of turning back to Me. I will always forgive you and will always justify you on the basis of the shed blood. As it says in Romans, you can stand in My Presence in joy knowing that you are justified.

VISION: I was at a class on "How to Hear God's Voice" and we were taking communion in a quiet and personally contemplative fashion. I began to see these scenes play across my imagination. I saw these scenes from the movie, *The Passion of the Christ.* Jesus was passing out the bread to His disciples — then the scene changed to Him being brutally whipped. Next, I saw Him pass the cup at Passover, then the scene changed to Him with bowed head and blood dripping from the crown of thorns. The scene changed again to heaven and the mercy seat. As Jesus poured out His blood between the cherubim, I saw it change to something like liquid gold. It was swirling like a golden tornado between the wings - glowing bright, valuable, precious, and enduring. Then I saw Jesus in red, royal robes, and He was completely radiant with golden glory. He was enthroned behind and above the mercy seat and was reigning over it.

Chapter Thirty-Two

THOUGHT LIFE

As a man thinketh in his heart so is he, not only embraces the whole of a man's being, but is so comprehensive as to reach out to every condition and circumstance of his life. A man is literally what he thinks, his character being the complete sum of all his thoughts.
—James Allen

Think, Think, Think, Pooh

Most of us don't think of our thoughts as an actual, physical component of our anatomy and biology. Perhaps our thoughts just seem like an ethereal stream of ideas or imagination or logic and reason, but not like a physical part of our DNA and brain. We may perceive thoughts as intangible, and lacking any material substance. However, I was surprised to learn that this is simply not the case. I am most definitely not a neuroscientist, but I have discovered some basic information about the power of thoughts, and that thoughts are one of the most powerful things that human beings possess.

Part of the training to become an educator requires a basic knowledge of cognitive development. I'm happy for that because the workings of the human brain fascinate me. I have been teaching Spanish in school for several decades, and I always tell my students that when they acquire a new language, it builds beautiful Spanish trees in their brains. I use the analogy of trees because our thoughts are made of proteins and these proteins look like trees in the brain.[4] In essence, the students' process of new language acquisition is giving them an enhanced brain. All the connections that they are forming and bridges that they are building within the anatomy of their brains create innumerable new complex structures.

Our brains are composed of billions of nerve cells (neurons), which are interconnected by trillions of electrochemical connections called synapses. Did you know that the human brain is designed with a special function of the frontal lobe to be able to screen every thought that arises within itself? This is called the Multiple Perspective Advantage (MPA). We can actually examine the thoughts that we are having and make a choice to accept or reject them. Think of it as something like taking a helicopter ride over a forest and getting a bird's eye view of each and every tree. Some of the trees are healthy, green and lush and some are toxic, dark and barren looking.

Hopefully as we learn to screen every thought, we will nurture the healthy thoughts and quickly disregard the negative thoughts. The advantage of doing this is huge. As we choose the physical proteins (thoughts) that we want to grow in our brain, that choice will determine whether we grow a healthy tree or an unhealthy one. It is general knowledge that research indicates that seventy-five to ninety-eight percent of current mental, physical, and behavioral illnesses today come from our thought life. That's powerful stuff!

I once had a teacher who often quoted Martin Luther, You cannot keep birds from flying over your head, but you can keep them from building a nest in your hair. My teacher used this saying to illustrate how to deal with negative thoughts. We may have negative thoughts that fly through our consciousness, but we don't have to let them become rooted in our thinking. A stronghold is built of thoughts, ideas, feelings, and evidence from circumstances until it becomes such a conviction and persuasion that one acts out one's life based on this constructed belief. Although it begins as a mental process, it ultimately becomes engrafted in the spirit of a man.[5]

Whispers of the Divine

You still need to learn the distinction between your thoughts, My thoughts, and the enemy's thoughts. Spend more time in My Word. Let it soak into you. Let it pervade your thinking. It is My Word that judges and sifts the intents and thoughts of the heart. It can be very incisive with regard to your thinking and shed light on the origin of thought. Hahaha! I created the brain, don't you know!? I know all about the biology, chemistry and electromagnetic functions of the brain! When you become conscious of your thinking, ask Me then to show you where the thoughts are coming from. Ask the Holy Spirit (your guide into all truth) to help you discern and be attentive to your thoughts. He will help you. Once you have learned to distinguish My voice more clearly, you will have the confidence to receive what I am telling you as wisdom from above, and it will set you free. My wisdom is pure, and peaceable, and it is easy to be reasoned with because it is truth. Truth always brings light, and light brings freedom.

I have revealed to you many times the importance of your thoughts and words. The economy of My Kingdom is based on believing and speaking. Therefore, what you think in your heart and say out of your mouth is what directs the course of your life, but it also can have an impact on the lives of others. That is why I am emphasizing it again in your life. You must know the importance of this reality in your life and you must strive to be disciplined in thought and in word to progress in relationship with Me. Remember when I told you sometime back that the course of your life for the future was going to require much discipline, but that it would be worth it? This is one of the facets of discipline I was referring to. So, be cautious before you speak. Check your heart to make sure the Holy Spirit is ok with what you are about to say. He is your guide into all truth. You are correct in observing that both I and the devil use words to accomplish our purposes. This is why it is imperative that you align with Me and My Word if you want to achieve My purposes in your life.

If I am big enough to fill the entire universe, and yet small enough to fill the tiniest part of the atomic microcosm, can I not fill even your thoughts? All things are created by My Words. My thoughts are filled with faith and then expressed through My breath outward in voice. My voice carries My Spirit, as does yours. Your voice carries your spirit. When your voice is also infused with faith in My power — My spirit — you will be able to express My power as you release My words. As I have told you many times, the key is meditating on my word and letting it be ingrafted in your spirit being. When the revelation of that word becomes conceived in your spirit, it is then a reality for you. As a man thinks in his heart so is he. As you conceive My realities in your heart, you will then think those thoughts, and you will be what you think. It happens not at a conscious level, but at a subconscious, or more accurately, spiritual level of your being. This is how I can help you, but you must help Me by receiving the ingrafted word which is able to save your soul. Take the time to do this. It is of the utmost importance.

When I create, it is not just form and thought. It is word — it is My breath, Myself that I put into my creation. The essence of Who I am exists in My creation. You are made in My image and likeness. You are more like Me than you think. So, think about it.

Chapter Thirty-Three

TIME

*Time, therefore, has its most real existence within our perception.
The only way in which your past still exists is in your memory. The
only way in which your future exists is in your anticipation. The
only way in which the present exists is in your awareness.*
— Andre Rabe

Tick Tock

One inevitable consequence of being an educator for over
four decades has is an acute mindfulness of time. Questions I
continually ask myself as a teacher go something like this: How
much time will it take to complete this lesson? What time are
recess and lunch? How much time should we spend on this
particular unit? When does this period begin and end? When is
my time sheet due? These are just a few of the constant questions
on the mind of one who manages students and tasks and time.
Trust me when I say that looking at the clock becomes an
ingrained habit.

The reality of time is that it is a gift daily dispensed equally
to each and every individual on planet Earth. Sometimes I think I
may have made time my master instead of allowing the Lord to be
the Master of my time. If I could freely allow the Infinite, Eternal
One to master time for me, then each moment could be loaded
with eternity. I could be more patient with myself and with others
because we are all changing in His Presence — line upon line,
precept upon precept, like the night changing to day or one season
becoming the next — gradually, almost imperceptibly.

Whispers of the Divine

*Be disciplined with your time — start with time. Redeem
the time — give value to your time. It is a gift; don't waste
it. Time is a resource and timing is a strategy. Bring
spiritual value into your time. I can save you time. When*

you get distracted you have to repeat things, which wastes time. When you remain focused you can be more efficient with your time.

You are too worried about time. Let go of time when you are with Me. I am outside of time. When you step into My presence you can let go of time. Accept instead the rhythm of my movement in you by the Spirit. Flow with Me; I know when to release you into your responsibilities. I will take care of you, My child. You are not alone in this world. I am ever with you, only a breath away, yours for the asking, yours for the taking. I will fill you up with goodness, My goodness.

Live in the present. Only the present is eternal for you because that is where I am. The past is gone and can never be relived (although it can be redeemed.) The future has not presented itself yet (although it can be prepared for). Live in the present. What you have done yesterday can influence your life, but your relationship with Me is in the present only. You cannot depend upon the successes of yesterday or the intentions of tomorrow when it comes to your response to Me. I am a NOW God — I live in eternity, which is always in the present. I am not talking about time; I am talking about the quality of being PRESENT in the now as though it counted for everything. Just as you have to be nourished nutritionally daily, and cannot depend upon the food of yesterday to nourish you today, so also you must be nourished by Me daily. That is why I gave the example of manna in the desert. What you receive from Me needs to be today. I told you recently that your responsibility is your ability to respond to Me. My responsibility is to respond to you with My ability — faith is now, obedience is now, hope is now, love is now. I am a NOW God. How you respond to Me now will determine the future outcome.

Chapter Thirty-Four

TRUST

Trust is earned when actions meet words.
—Chris Butler

Let Go, and Let God

We come into this world naked and helpless. We are unable to care for ourselves in any way, shape or form. We hardly know anything at all except what we can feel. We cannot feed ourselves, or clothe ourselves or move around to find comfort in our surroundings. We have literally just been violently ejected from the only home we've ever known. We are utterly dependent and in a position to have to trust our parents or other caretakers.

The Bible has a definite perspective about our arrival into this world, and what the purpose is for this vulnerable season. Psalm 22:9 says: "But You are He who took Me out of the womb; You made Me trust while on My mother's breasts." We begin our life on earth learning to trust, because the quality of our relationship with our Creator will be entirely dependent upon our ability to trust Him.

At the time of this writing, I have been teaching for forty-four years and counting. Over the expanse of these more than four decades, my experience has ranged from preschool through college. So you could say that I have gone through every phase of child development and beyond. Through the years, I have noticed a thing or two relating to people and trust.

My three- and four-year-old preschoolers instinctively trust the adults who care for them, both parents and teachers. When we tell them something, they take us at our word and believe us. Even more than that, when we say that we are going to do something, they will continually remind us until we make good on our word. They know that they don't know a whole lot, and that we do, so they trust us and expect us to care for them.

As children grow and develop and learn more and more about life, they become increasingly independent and less dependent upon the adults in their world. Eventually, in college and beyond they move into adulthood. Perhaps somewhere along the way circumstances have revealed that not all adults can be trusted or depended upon. In any case, many of us become stunted in our capacity to trust in the same childlike way we did in our formative years.

When we come into a relationship with our Heavenly Father by accepting Christ into our life, we are spiritually born again and begin a brand new walk of trust and faith in One who we cannot see. In this new spiritual relationship, we will have to unlearn all the defense mechanisms, independent ways, and other hindrances to developing intimacy with our Creator. Trust is the bridge that connects the human with the Divine.

Whispers of the Divine

Trust comes with experience. You know the prayer in Ephesians that speaks of knowing the height, breadth, length and depth of God's love that goes past understanding because it comes from experience. Intimacy is about engaging and experiencing the one with whom you desire to be close. Again, as repetitive as it sounds, spending time with Me is the one, true way to experience Me. As you allow My Spirit to reveal My nature to you, and bring understanding to My Word for you, you begin to know Me more and more. So, again I must encourage you to sit quietly with Me — no agenda, not to complete a task, assignment, etc. — just to BE with Me, and let Me take the lead in the conversation. As I share with you in those moments and you see My words to you come to fulfillment, your trust in Me will deepen. You have experienced this some in the past, but the more You allow Me to lead in this process, the stronger your faith and trust will become.

Oh, the plans I have for your life! Joy awaits you! Peace awaits you! Love awaits you! How do you learn to trust someone? You allow them to see the real you, and when they accept who you are just as you are, you begin to trust in their love for you. I have accepted who you are just as you are from the beginning. I know all about you, every detail of your life from the beginning to the end, and I have embraced you in My Son from before the foundation of the world. Oh, the glorious plans I have for your life! Rest, My child. Rest in My love. I have told you to strive only to enter into My rest. Let all your effort be toward that. Work only to enter into the rest that I have provided for you.

Trust. You think that someday when all the activity of your life has slowed down that then you'll be able to rest. Not so. I was at rest in the midst of the storm, and you can be at rest in a flurry of activity. You are not in charge! I am in charge, and I don't need your help. Resting is an indication of a heart condition called trust. Learn to trust Me. Practice trusting Me. Practice letting go. Remember my admonition: Trust in the Lord with all your heart and lean not to your own understanding. In all your ways acknowledge Him, and He will direct your paths. Come and be with Me awhile.

Chapter Thirty -Five

TRUTH

Truth is valuable, and it prevails.
—Sojourner Truth

The Infinite Perspective

Is truth the ability to perceive reality in the most correct form, free from any tainted perceptions or bias? There is only One who can see everything rightly, because only He knows the end from the beginning and has the infinite perspective, knowledge and understanding to know what is truly right. So great is His faithfulness that it is impossible for Him to lie. That being so, we should pursue His view of reality and allow what He knows to be truth to permeate our perspective. Truth is the highest reality.

We may think that we even know ourselves in truth. The reality is that we can be self-deceived. There is an interesting chart that outlines four categories of how we see ourselves as human beings:

♦ We see what others do not see.

♦ Others see what we do not see.

♦ We see and others see.

♦ We do not see, nor do others see.

However, God sees ALL!

Whispers of the Divine

I am the way, the truth, and the life. Everything that I do and say is replete with truth. Theology can be truth, but just as the Word without the Spirit can be death and destructive, so theology without the corresponding relationship to Me can be dead religion. My words are spirit AND truth. Theology as it pertains to truth is valuable, but theology as a stand alone is dangerous. One can be deceived into thinking that he knows God, when in reality he only knows things about God. Such thinking can even be opposed to God because it becomes so far removed from the character of the One behind the truth. This has been illustrated many times in Scripture in my confrontation with the religious leaders of My time. They were so persuaded of their truths about God that they missed the very One sent to them from God the Father.

Chapter Thirty-Six

WAITING vs WORKING

*I try to remember that walking in the will of God might mean
waiting as much as it might mean moving forward.*
—Tessa Afshar

Read the Red and Pray the Power

When I think about the fact that I am intended to be like
Jesus Christ, it is quite overwhelming! How could I possibly live
up to such a stature? Then, I realize that conformity to Christ can
only happen as I spend time with Him to see what He is like in
every circumstance of life. As I meditate on His life in the
scriptures and allow His Holy Spirit to breathe inspiration and
revelation into my understanding, I am able to receive the grace
of transformation.

For this reason, I like to do what I call read the red and pray
the power. Some Bibles have the words of Jesus in red, so I read
what Jesus is saying, observe what He is doing, and pray for the
power of God to help me live in the same way.

On one particular occasion as I was doing this, I was
impressed with the fact that Jesus never did anything in ministry
until it was time. Even when in fact the hour had come to begin
His ministry, He yielded in obedience to be baptized by John, and
filled with the Holy Spirit. Did He immediately jump into healing
the sick and preaching in the synagogues? No. He was led into the
wilderness to be tempted by the devil. Spending time alone in the
desert with the devil for forty days would not be my first choice
for the start of a ministry!

Even though Jesus was anointed, His first act of ministry
was to overcome the strongman before He went teaching,
preaching and healing. He had to bow down in obedience to the
Father and overcome the three areas of temptation that Adam and
Eve had yielded to in the Garden of Eden — lust of the eyes, lust

of the flesh, and pride of life. What I saw that day as I lingered in this portion of scripture was that I should never do the works before I do the appropriate waiting in worship.

Whispers of the Divine

I laid aside My dignity as God in order to show you how to live in dependence upon the Father. The Father is great and mighty and preeminent in all things. All things came from Him. Life comes from Him. Nothing is possible without Him, but all things are possible with Him, in Him, and through Him. Surely if I chose to be entirely dependent upon Him even though I was with Him in the beginning, you can see the necessity for you to be utterly dependent upon Him. Whether you realize it or not, you truly are. Give your heart to Him on a daily basis. Take time to be in His Presence early as I did. Wait upon Him, realizing it is futile to go forward in your own strength. Worship Him. Wait upon Him. Wait upon Him. Waiting is action in the spirit of yielding, releasing, bowing, praising, remembering, rehearsing, worshiping, forgiving, receiving — whatever and however the Spirit leads you in His Presence. It is actively submitting to the will of the Father. This takes internal adjustments — heart adjustments. Waiting is actively giving your heart to the Father and allowing Him to fill it with His dreams for you. Remember in the Word it says that you are His workmanship, for the works prepared beforehand by Him. When you wait on Him, you will discover what those works are. Then and only then can you successfully do the works.

You have supposed that it is I who want you to do for Me — that I somehow demand doing from you. Nothing could be further from the truth. It is I who want to do for you. I just want you to be and receive what I have done. I do the doing — you do the responding. It is like a dance — I lead, you follow, and we both move to the music of the Spirit. You only have to lean on Me to do the dance.

Chapter Thirty-Seven

WORSHIP

Worship is giving God the best that He has given you.
—Oswald Chambers

Drawing Near

One of my routines for self-care that always lifts me up and makes me feel better is to get a mani-pedi. For you gentlemen readers who don't know– that means getting one's nails done on both hands and feet (manicure/pedicure.) I don't know if it is like this in other areas, but I live in Southern California, and here it is most common for the nail salons to be owned and managed by beautiful Vietnamese people.

When I walk into one of these nail salons, there is always a shrine with a Buddha sitting and surrounded by flowers and incense and offerings of fruit or a big cookie. This is worship. These offerings are the vehicles for the people to draw near to their deity. It is their means of sacrifice. Jesus said to the woman at the well in Samaria, Many worship what they do not know.

When the word *sacrifice* appears in the Bible, it is from a Hebrew root word, *corban (kor'-ban, qorban; doron)* which is translated "a gift; a sacrificial offering," literally, "that which is brought near," namely, to the altar.[6] This word means more or less to draw near. Jesus mentions this word in Mark 7:11 when He is pointing out to the Pharisees that they are using *corban* as an excuse to not provide and care for their parents.

The Bible mentions many ways we can draw near to God: through the fruit of our lips in worship; giving thanks; acting in obedience to His Word; or bringing an actual offering. Each one of these done with a heart rendered to God is our worship to Him. We no longer bring our physical sacrifices to a physical altar, because Jesus, the Lamb of God, has poured out His living blood on the heavenly mercy seat. He was the once and for all Living Sacrifice.

When I walk into the nail salon and see the altar to Buddha, I am reminded that I don't worship a statue who sits there and can't smell incense and who doesn't eat fruit or a cookie! I worship Jesus who is alive! He is alive and has all power and authority in His hands! He arose in glory with all power and authority! He conquered my enemies and He put them under my feet! I worship the living God in and through my spirit, in which His Holy Spirit now lives and forever shall be with me throughout all eternity. Worship is the best self-care ever!

Whispers of the Divine

What is left of the synagogue in Capernaum, a place of worship in Israel? Some stones, some pillars? Do you remember what I said to the woman at the well in Samaria? Many worship what they do not know. The Jews did worship what they knew for they had a covenant with the Father. But now, true worshippers will worship in spirit and in truth — that is what the Father seeks. The closer you draw to Me, the closer you are to truth, for I am Truth. You must worship in truth, and the Spirit of Truth leads the way, for He leads and guides you into all Truth. Seek Me, seek truth, and you will find the Father. Allow the Holy Spirit to continually flow within you and through you, lifting your heart in worship. This is well-pleasing to the Father. It is in truth that the Kingdom is established in the heart of man. It cannot be otherwise.

Appendix A

This author is hopeful that you have been able to hear the sound of God's voice speaking to you as you have journeyed through these writings. His voice is so kind and wise — sometimes humorous, and sometimes given to challenge growth where we have become stuck. Always, His voice is brilliant and wonderful beyond all our expectations.

I have been journaling my devotional times since 1980. Over the years I've filled numerous journals, recording my thoughts, feelings, and my dialogs with God. However, this practice took a quantum leap in 2012 when I was attending a class on How to Hear God's Voice presented by a couple who are in leadership at my church.

The impact of learning the simplicity and frequency with which one could hear God talking to us was transformational! Instead of being a random occurrence, over which one has no particular control, hearing God speak to us in our hearts becomes something that could happen on a regular and ongoing basis if we would follow just four simple keys to hearing God's voice. The following is information on doing just that from the book, *Four Steps to Hearing God's Voice*, by Dr. Mark Virkler, and his wife, Patti Virkler.

How to Hear God's Voice — By Dr. Mark Virkler

She had done it again! Instead of coming straight home from school like she was supposed to, she had gone to her friend's house. Without permission. Without our knowledge. Without doing her chores.

With a ministering household that included remnants of three struggling families plus our own toddler and newborn, my wife simply couldn't handle all the work on her own. Everyone had to pull their own weight. Everyone had age-appropriate tasks they were expected to complete. At fourteen, Rachel and her younger brother were living with us while her parents tried to overcome lifestyle patterns that had resulted in the children running away to escape the dysfunction. I felt sorry for Rachel, but, honestly my wife was my greatest concern.

Now Rachel had ditched her chores to spend time with her friends. It wasn't the first time, but if I had anything to say about it, it would be the last. I intended to lay down the law when she got home and make it very clear that if she was going to live under my roof, she would obey my rules.

But she wasn't home yet. And I had recently been learning to hear God's voice more clearly. Maybe I should try to see if I could hear anything from Him about the situation. Maybe He could give me a way to get her to do what she was supposed to (i.e. what I wanted her to do). So I went to my office and reviewed what the Lord had been teaching me from Habakkuk 2:1,2: I will stand on my guard post and station myself on the rampart; And I will keep watch to see what He will speak to me...Then the Lord answered me and said, 'Record the vision....'

Habakkuk said, I will stand on my guard post... (Hab. 2:1). **The first key to hearing God's voice is to go to a quiet place and still our own thoughts and emotions.** Psalm 46:10 encourages us to be still, let go, cease striving, and know that He is God. In Psalm 37:7 we are called to be still before the Lord and wait patiently for Him. There is a deep inner knowing in our spirits that each of us can experience when we quiet our flesh and our minds. Practicing the art of biblical meditation helps silence the outer noise and distractions clamoring for our attention.

I didn't have a guard post but I did have an office, so I went there to quiet my temper and my mind. Loving God through a quiet worship song is one very effective way to become still. In 2 Kings 3, Elisha needed a word from the Lord so he said, Bring me a minstrel, and as the minstrel played, the Lord spoke. I have found that playing a worship song on my autoharp is the quickest way for me to come to stillness. I need to choose my song carefully; boisterous songs of praise do not bring me to stillness, but rather gentle songs that express my love and worship. And it isn't enough just to sing the song into the cosmos — I come into the Lord's presence most quickly and easily when I use my godly imagination to see the truth that He is right here with me and I sing my songs to Him, personally.

I will keep watch to see, said the prophet. To receive the pure word of God, it is very important that my heart be properly focused as I become still, because my focus is the source of the intuitive flow. If I fix my eyes upon Jesus (Heb. 12:2), the intuitive flow comes from Jesus. But if I fix my gaze upon some desire of my heart, the intuitive flow comes out of that desire. To have a pure flow I must become still and carefully fix my eyes upon Jesus. Quietly worshiping the King and receiving out of the stillness that follows quite easily accomplishes this.

So I used **the second key to hearing God's voice: As you pray, fix the eyes of your heart upon Jesus, seeing in the Spirit the dreams and visions of Almighty God.** Habakkuk was actually looking for vision as he prayed. He opened the eyes of his heart, and looked into the spirit world to see what God wanted to show him.

God has always spoken through dreams and visions, and He specifically said that they would come to those upon whom the Holy Spirit is poured out (Acts 2:1-4, 17).

Being a logical, rational person, observable facts that could be verified by my physical senses were the foundations of my life, including my spiritual life. I had never thought of opening the eyes of my heart and looking for vision. However, I have come to believe that this is exactly what God wants me to do. He gave me eyes in my heart to see in the spirit the vision and movement of Almighty God. There is an active spirit world all around us, full of angels, demons, the Holy Spirit, the omnipresent Father, and His omnipresent Son, Jesus. The only reasons for me not to see this reality are unbelief or lack of knowledge.

In his sermon in Acts 2:25, Peter refers to King David's statement: I saw the Lord always in my presence; for He is at my right hand, so that I will not be shaken. The original psalm makes it clear that this was a decision of David's, not a constant supernatural visitation: I have set (literally, I have placed) the Lord continually before me; because He is at my right hand, I will not be shaken (Ps.16:8). Because David knew that the Lord was always with him, he determined in his spirit to *see* that truth with the eyes of his heart as he went through life, knowing that this would keep his faith strong.

In order to see, we must look. Daniel saw a vision in his mind and said, I was looking...I kept looking...I kept looking (Dan. 7:2, 9, 13). As I pray, I look for Jesus, and I watch as He speaks to me, doing and saying the things that are on His heart. Many Christians will find that if they will only look, they will see. Jesus is Emmanuel, God with us (Matt. 1:23). It is as simple as that. You can see Christ present with you because Christ *is* present with you. In fact, the vision may come so easily that you will be tempted to reject it, thinking that it is just you. But if you persist in recording these visions, your doubt will soon be overcome by faith as you recognize that the content of them could only be birthed in Almighty God.

Jesus demonstrated the ability of living out of constant contact with God, declaring that He did nothing on His own initiative, but only what He saw the Father doing, and heard the Father saying (Jn. 5:19,20,30). What an incredible way to live!

Is it possible for us to live out of divine initiative as Jesus did? Yes! We must simply fix our eyes upon Jesus. The veil has been torn, giving access into the immediate presence of God, and He calls us to draw near (Lk. 23:45; Heb. 10:19-22). I pray that the eyes of your heart will be enlightened....

When I had quieted my heart enough that I was able to picture Jesus without the distractions of my own ideas and plans, I was able to keep watch to see what He will speak to me. I wrote down my question: Lord, what should I do about Rachel?

Immediately the thought came to me, She is insecure. Well, that certainly wasn't my thought! Her behavior looked like rebellion to me, not insecurity.

But like Habakkuk, I was coming to know the sound of God speaking to me (Hab. 2:2). Elijah described it as a still, small voice (I Kings 19:12). I had previously listened for an inner audible voice, and God does speak that way at times. However, I have found that usually, God's voice comes as spontaneous thoughts, visions, feelings, or impressions.

For example, haven't you been driving down the road and had a thought come to you to pray for a certain person? Didn't you believe it was God telling you to pray? What did God's voice sound like? Was it an audible voice, or was it a spontaneous thought that lit upon your mind?

Experience indicates that we perceive spirit-level communication as spontaneous thoughts, impressions and visions, and Scripture confirms this in many ways. For example, one definition of *paga*, a Hebrew word for intercession, is a chance encounter or an accidental intersecting. When God lays people on our hearts, He does it through *paga*, a chance-encounter thought accidentally intersecting our minds.

So **the third key to hearing God's voice is recognizing that God's voice in your heart often sounds like a flow of spontaneous thoughts.** Therefore, when I want to hear from God, I tune to chance-encounter or spontaneous thoughts.

Finally, God told Habakkuk to record the vision (Hab. 2:2). This was not an isolated command. The Scriptures record many examples of individual's prayers and God's replies, such as the Psalms, many of the prophets, and Revelation. I have found that obeying this final principle amplified my confidence in my ability to hear God's voice so that I could finally make living out of His initiatives a way of life. The **fourth key, two-way journaling or the writing out of your prayers and God's answers, brings great freedom in hearing God's voice.**

I have found two-way journaling to be a fabulous catalyst for clearly discerning God's inner, spontaneous flow, because as I journal I am able to write in faith for long periods of time, simply believing it is God. I know that what I believe I have received from God must be tested. However, testing involves doubt and doubt blocks divine communication, so I do not want to test while I am trying to receive. (See James 1:5-8.) With journaling, I can receive in faith, knowing that when the flow has ended I can test and examine it carefully.

So I wrote down what I believed He had said: She is insecure.But the Lord wasn't done. I continued to write the spontaneous thoughts that came to me: Love her unconditionally. She is flesh of your flesh and bone of your bone.

My mind immediately objected: She is not flesh of my flesh. She is not related to me at all — she is a foster child, just living in my home temporarily. It was definitely time to test this word from the Lord!

There are three possible sources of thoughts in our minds: ourselves, satan and the Holy Spirit. It was obvious that the words in my journal did not come from my own mind — I certainly didn't see her as insecure *or* flesh of my flesh. And I sincerely doubted that Satan would encourage me to love anyone unconditionally!

Okay, it was starting to look like I might have actually received counsel from the Lord. It was consistent with the names and character of God as revealed in the Scripture, and totally contrary to the names and character of the enemy. So that meant that I was hearing from the Lord, and He wanted me to see the situation in a different light. Rachel was my daughter — part of my family not by blood but by the hand of God Himself. The chaos of her birth home had created deep insecurity about her worthiness to be loved by anyone, including me and including God. Only the unconditional love of the Lord expressed through an imperfect human would reach her heart.

But there was still one more test I needed to perform before I would have absolute confidence that this was truly God's word to me: I needed confirmation from someone else whose spiritual discernment I trusted. So I went to my wife and shared what I had received. I knew if I could get her validation, especially since she was the one most wronged in the situation, then I could say, at least to myself, Thus sayeth the Lord.

Needless to say, Patti immediately and without question confirmed that the Lord had spoken to me. My entire planned lecture was forgotten. I returned to my office anxious to hear more. As the Lord planted a new, supernatural love for Rachel within me, He showed me what to say and how to say it to not only address the current issue of household responsibility, but the deeper issues of love and acceptance and worthiness.

Rachel and her brother remained as part of our family for another two years, giving us many opportunities to demonstrate and teach about the Father's love, planting spiritual seeds in thirsty soil. We weren't perfect and we didn't solve all of her issues, but because I had learned to listen to the Lord, we were able to avoid creating more brokenness and separation.

The four simple keys that the Lord showed me from Habakkuk have been used by people of all ages, from four to a hundred and four, from every continent, culture and denomination, to break through into intimate two-way conversations with their loving Father and dearest Friend. Omitting any one of the keys will prevent you from receiving all He wants to say to you. The order of the keys is not important, just that you *use them all*. Embracing all four, by faith, can change your life. Simply quiet yourself down, tune to spontaneity, look for vision, and journal. He is waiting to meet you there.

You will be amazed when you journal! Doubt may hinder you at first, but throw it off, reminding yourself that it is a biblical concept, and that God is present, speaking to His children. Relax. When we cease our labors and enter His rest, God is free to flow (Heb. 4:10).

Why not try it for yourself, right now? Sit back comfortably, take out your pen and paper, and smile. Turn your attention toward the Lord in praise and worship, seeking His face. Many people have found the music and visionary prayer called A Stroll Along the Sea of Galilee helpful in getting them started. You can listen to it and download it free at **www.CWGMinistries.org/Galilee**.

After you write your question to Him, become still, fixing your gaze on Jesus. You will suddenly have a very good thought. Don't doubt it; simply write it down. Later, as you read your journaling, you, too, will be blessed to discover that you are indeed dialoguing with God. If you wonder if it is really the Lord speaking to you, share it with your spouse or a friend. Their input will encourage your faith and strengthen your commitment to spend time getting to know the Lover of your soul more intimately than you ever dreamed possible.

Is It *Really* God?

Five ways to be sure what you're hearing is from Him:

1) Test the Origin (1 Jn. 4:1)
Thoughts from our own minds are progressive, with one thought leading to the next, however tangentially. Thoughts from the spirit world are spontaneous. The Hebrew word for true prophecy is *naba,* which literally means to bubble up, whereas false prophecy is *ziyd* meaning to boil up. True words from the Lord will bubble up from our innermost being; we don't need to cook them up ourselves.

2) Compare It to Biblical Principles
God will never say something to you personally which is contrary to His universal revelation as expressed in the Scriptures. If the Bible clearly states that something is a sin, no amount of journaling can make it right. Much of what you journal about will not be specifically addressed in the Bible, however, so an understanding of biblical principles is also needed.

3) Compare It to the Names and Character of God as Revealed in the Bible
Anything God says to you will be in harmony with His essential nature. Journaling will help you get to *know* God

personally, but knowing what the Bible says *about* Him will help you discern what words are from Him. Make sure the tenor of your journaling lines up with the character of God as described in the names of the Father, Son and Holy Spirit.

4) Test the Fruit (Matt. 7:15-20)

What effect does what you are hearing have on your soul and your spirit? Words from the Lord will quicken your faith and increase your love, peace and joy. They will stimulate a sense of humility within you as you become more aware of Who God is and who you are. On the other hand, any words you receive which cause you to fear or doubt, which bring you into confusion or anxiety, or which stroke your ego (especially if you hear something that is just for you alone — no one else is worthy) must be immediately rebuked and rejected as lies of the enemy.

5) Share It with Your Spiritual Counselors (Prov. 11:14)

We are members of a Body! A cord of three strands is not easily broken and God's intention has always been for us to grow together. Nothing will increase your faith in your ability to hear from God like having it confirmed by two or three other people! Share it with your spouse, your parents, your friends, your elder, your group leader, even your grown children can be your sounding board. They don't need to be perfect or super-spiritual; they just need to love you, be committed to being available to you, have a solid biblical orientation, and most importantly, they must also willingly and easily receive counsel. Avoid the authoritarian who insists that because of their standing in the church or with God, they no longer need to listen to others. Find two or three people and let them confirm that you are hearing from God!

The book *4 Keys to Hearing God's Voice* is available at **www.CWGMinistries.org**.

Notes

1 Isaiah 46:9-10 (KJV): 9 Remember the former things of old: for I am God, and there is none else; I am God, and there is none like me,10 Declaring the end from the beginning, and from ancient times the things that are not yet done, saying, My counsel shall stand, and I will do all my pleasure.

2 2 John 3:3 (AMPC) Jesus answered him, I assure you, most solemnly I tell you, that unless a person is born again (anew, from above), he cannot ever see (know, be acquainted with, and experience) the kingdom of God.

3 Ephesians 2:4-6 (NIV) 4 But because of his great love for us, God, who is rich in mercy, 5 made us alive with Christ even when we were dead in transgressions—it is by grace you have been saved. 6 And God raised us up with Christ and seated us with him in the heavenly realms in Christ Jesus.

4https://www.psychologytoday.com/us/articles/200301/brain-power-why-proteins-are-smart

5 2 Corinthians 10:3-6 (VOICE) 3 For though we walk in the world, we do not fight according to this world's rules of warfare. 4 The weapons of the war we're fighting are not of this world but are powered by God and effective at tearing down the strongholds erected against His truth. 5 We are demolishing arguments and ideas, every high-and-mighty philosophy that pits itself against the knowledge of the one true God. We are taking prisoners of every thought, every emotion, and subduing them into obedience to the Anointed One. 6 As soon as you choose obedience, we stand ready to punish every act of disobedience.

6 Orr, James, M.A., D.D. General Editor. Entry for "corban." International Standard Bible Encyclopedia. 1915.